CONTEMPORARY
Loom Beading

CONTEMPORARY

Loom Beading

A NEW LOOK AT A TRADITIONAL STITCH

Sharon Bateman

LARK BOOKS

A Division of Sterling Publishing Co., Inc.

New York / London

Senior Editor
Terry Taylor

Editor
Linda Kopp

Assistant Editor
Amanda Carestio

Technical Editor
Chris Rich

Book Design
828, Inc.

Photographer
Lynne Harty

Cover Designer
Chris Bryant

Bateman, Sharon, 1960-
  Contemporary loom beading: a new look at a traditional stitch / Sharon Bateman. -- 1st ed.
    p. cm.
  Includes index.
  ISBN 978-1-60059-273-7 (hc-plc with jacket : alk. paper)
  1. Beadwork. 2. Handlooms. I. Title.
  TT860.B33367 2009
  745.58'2--dc22

10 9 8 7 6 5 4 3 2 1

First Edition

Published by Lark Books, A Division of
Sterling Publishing Co., Inc.
387 Park Avenue South, New York, NY 10016

Text and Illustrations © 2009, Sharon Bateman
Photography © 2009, Lark Books

Distributed in Canada by Sterling Publishing,
c/o Canadian Manda Group, 165 Dufferin Street
Toronto, Ontario, Canada M6K 3H6

Distributed in the United Kingdom by GMC Distribution Services,
Castle Place, 166 High Street, Lewes, East Sussex, England BN7 1XU

Distributed in Australia by Capricorn Link (Australia) Pty Ltd.,
P.O. Box 704, Windsor, NSW 2756 Australia

If you have questions or comments about this book, please contact:
Lark Books
67 Broadway
Asheville, NC 28801
828-253-0467

Manufactured in China

ISBN 13: 978-1-60059-273-7

For information about custom editions, special sales, premium and corporate purchases, please contact Sterling Special Sales Department at 800-805-5489 or specialsales@sterlingpub.com.

contents

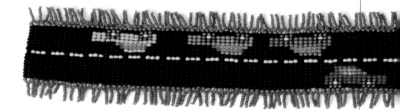

introduction

I was introduced to beadwork when I found a little wire loom under the Christmas tree. It turned out to be a much more useful and life-changing gift than the Easy Bake Oven (which mysteriously disappeared shortly after I set it on fire trying to make a faux amber pendant out of an empty pill bottle).

Wire looms just like my first loom can still be found on shelves in craft stores. They have been responsible for keeping loom work alive since the early 1900s. This type of loom (like the one shown on page 9 with the picture of the Indian chief on it) is small and kind of flimsy, but it has helped keep the rich history of beading on a loom alive. Using one of these looms—even as a child—is practically a rite of passage into the world of beadwork and can lead to a lifetime of creativity and pleasure.

Where some people might shy away from working with seed beads, those of us who love these small beauties revel in the process. Each moment is a pleasure where time is transcended, and in the end we have something beautiful to show for it.

In the past, beads came in limited, generally primary colors and were so uneven that you spent almost as much time culling the bad beads as you did weaving the good. This is not the case today. The quality of the beads has vastly improved over the last several years. They are more uniform with an astounding array of colors to complement any palette. Threads, too, come in a greater variety of materials and color.

Loom weaving may seem difficult, with lots of steps, but it can be easy if you know how. I'll show you the basic steps and some new tricks and tips that will have you beading like a pro in no time at all: tips like a sliding stop bead to hold your first row in place to make it easier; or conditioning your wax so it doesn't stress your thread. Did you know that you could use a darning needle to weave the ends of the warp threads? This one tip alone will save you hours and make finishing your work incredibly easy.

With today's materials, Victorian watch fobs, tribal regalia, and western hatbands are not all that you can create with loom beading. You can apply this traditional craft to some decidedly modern applications. How about a designer case for your cell phone (page 94) or MP3 player (page 120)? Buck the dehumanizing corporate system with a personalized lanyard for your security card (page 110). You can complement your decor with elegant light or fan pulls or geometric-patterned napkin rings (pages 88 and 82), and coasters so pretty everyone will actually want to use them (page 85). Jewelry is so easy to make, you'll be making coveted gifts for every occasion.

The projects in this book cover a wide variety of styles and interests, with a little something for everyone, from the beginner to the experienced beader. The possibilities for creativity with seed beads and a simple bead loom are endless, and I know you will enjoy making them as much as you enjoy the finished projects.

basics

Early 1900s beadwork

Glass in its natural state has existed since the earth began and has been worked for thousands of years. The art of glassblowing started in Syria around 100 B.C., spread throughout Europe, and was refined in Venice, where *seed beads*, made by slicing hollow glass tubes, were introduced between A.D. 1200 and 1400. Seed beads usually served as surface embellishment on fabrics and on crocheted or knitted purses.

By A.D. 1700, seed beads had been introduced to the native peoples of the Americas, who applied them as surface embellishments very much like quillwork. Native Americans originated the loom stitch, weaving *wampum beads* (beads made from shells) together in much the same way as loom work is done today. Belts and straps of wampum beads were made not only for decoration but as tangible memorials to important events such as treaties. These belts are not only beautiful but they also document the history of Native American peoples.

Native American beadwork, with its vibrant colors and simple, straightforward designs, celebrated the rich, intricate, spiritual, and political life that inspired it. By the 1800s, it was so popular and so well done that for many people it was—and still is—the very symbol of what beadwork

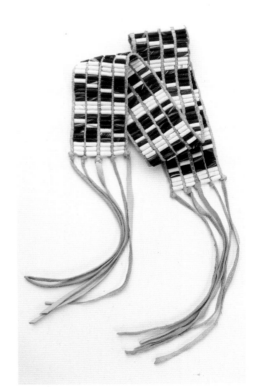

Belt with wampum beads

Native American spirit stick

is about. It often overshadows the complex European work that was popular in the 1800s and early 1900s, the rich variety of color and complex designs of which celebrated a straightforward and simple pleasure in beauty for beauty's sake. Both types of beadwork showed the status of the bearer, as well as the incredible vision and skill of the artisans. And each style was a reflection of the other, symbolizing the pride and passion these cultures had for themselves and one another.

So common was Native American beadwork that the word "Indian" became a logo of sorts for the commercialization of bead craft and the loom in particular. (The looms of those days had evolved from a bow-like tool made from a slightly curved tree limb to the Ojibwa-style loom made with boards and dowels.) Examples of such looms include the 1910 Apache loom and the Walco loom that is still marketed today.

Contemporary loom work is a combination of both Native American and European influences on traditional beadwork. With the work we produce today, we can reflect the best of both styles while taking advantage of modern materials. We have the freedom to acknowledge the past, while adding our own visions and passions.

Components of an antique purse

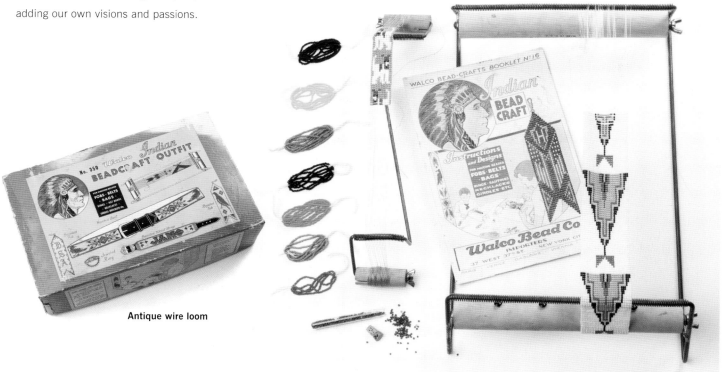

Antique wire loom

Most people are familiar with the looms used to weave fabrics. Looms for beadwork are essentially the same; they support *warp threads*—the threads that form the framework of a project. The length and width of your beadwork will be defined by how many warp threads you string and how long they are. Both factors will be limited by the size of your loom. You'll need a loom that is longer than the desired length of your woven piece, or one with rollers on which to wind the warp threads in order to store the extra length out of the way as you work.

Loom Anatomy

Every loom has components that help define its type and the dimensions of the beadwork that can be woven on it.

The *body* or *frame* defines the length of the loom. At each end of the body is a *bridge* that defines the width of the loom and supports the warp threads.

Spacers hold the warp threads in place and evenly spaced along the top of each bridge. The spacers can consist of notches cut into the bridge itself, the spiral-cut threads along a length of "all thread," or springs attached horizontally to both bridges.

Anchors are the hooks or screws at each end of a loom that hold the ends of the warp threads in place.

The *work space* is the span between the bridges, where the warp threads are suspended and the *weft threads*, onto which the beads are strung, are added. (Weft threads bind the beads to the framework formed by the warp threads.)

Types of Looms

SLEIGH LOOM—Named for its sleigh-like shape, this type of loom has a frame with a bridge at each end. The sleigh loom shown [below] is a good example.

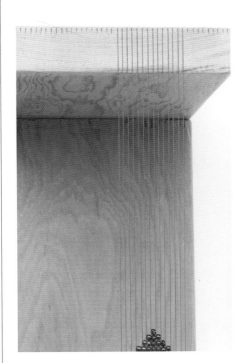

Spacers keep the warp threads in place and evenly spaced.

Anchors secure the warp thread ends.

A small, adjustable sleigh loom works well for small projects.

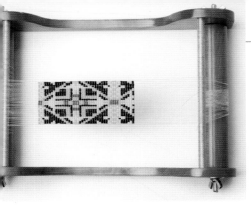

Professional beading loom (roller variety), available at many bead stores and outlets.

Disposable pin loom

Sharondipity looms

ROLLER LOOM—At each end of this type of loom is a roller onto which the threads and beadwork are rolled to keep them out of the way.

Both sleigh and roller looms can be used either vertically or horizontally. A vertical loom stands with its top or bottom bridge balanced in the lap or on a table so that the warp threads are perpendicular to the work surface. A horizontal loom sits with its bridges resting on a table; its working threads run parallel to the work surface.

DISPOSABLE LOOMS—Handmade from cardboard or foam board, disposable looms offer an easy way to try out the loom stitch before you spend money on a better loom. The *pin loom*, which is easy to construct with common materials, is a quick way to start. Instructions for making your own pin loom, as well as a durable wooden loom, are provided on page 140.

SHARONDIPITY LOOMS—For making specific projects (amulet bags and bracelets) without having any warp threads to tie off or weave in after you've completed the bead work, I designed the Tube Loom, Tiny Tube Loom, and Bracelet Loom. A completed amulet bag slides off the loom in a tube shape, which you can sew closed along one end. Adding fringe and a strap completes the process. The bracelet-loom projects are bangle-like endless straps that create their own safety catches when the clasps are added.

Selecting a Loom

When choosing a loom, the three most important factors to consider are your personality, the area in which you plan to work, and the sizes of the projects you intend to create.

For me, the most important personal question is "Can I walk away from my loom quickly?" I much prefer horizontal tabletop looms. I don't like vertical looms that rest in the lap because you have to put them down before you can get up and step away. I'm a fidgety person, so this causes me no end of grief. (Anyone with kids, grandkids, or a terrier of any kind will understand this!) Many people prefer the lap loom because it brings their work in closer, making it easier to see and manipulate, but a lap loom does require you to sit fairly still while balancing it on your lap.

If you live in a small place, such as an apartment or RV, you'll want a small loom or a roller loom that is compact and is easy to put away. If you have plenty of room and like to spread out, you may prefer a large loom; it takes up more space but allows you to see the whole project in progress.

If you're an experienced beader, take a moment to think about what types of projects appeal to you. Small projects such as bracelets can be made on a small loom, while large projects—wall hangings and elaborate split-loom necklaces for example—require a larger loom. Here's a good rule of thumb: Choose a loom that is half again as long and twice as wide as the largest project you've made to date. I'd recommend a roller loom. It's more versatile than other types since it doesn't limit the length of your projects, it's portable, and it doesn't take up much work space.

If you're new to beading, a small, inexpensive loom or a disposable one will give you a chance to see if you like loom beading before you make a large financial investment. A small loom will limit your project size, but until you're comfortable with the loom stitch, small projects will most likely be what you're interested in creating.

BEADS

Many varieties of beads are readily available at craft and bead stores, as well as online.

Types of Seed Beads

Weaving on a bead loom is done with seed beads of various sizes. These beads, which can be purchased in tubes or hanks, come in some common sizes, ranging from 15/0 through 4/0 (the larger the number, the smaller the bead).

JAPANESE AND CZECH SEED BEADS—These popular types of beads are named for their countries of origin. Each is made in different sizes and styles, and each lends a different appearance and size to a finished piece of loomed beadwork. The smaller the size of the bead, the more beads per square inch there will be in your finished work. Beads work in much the same way as pixels do in a digital image; the finer the beads, the better the quality of the picture.

Japanese beads are typically available in two sizes: 11/0 and 15/0. They're

shaped like marshmallows and have good-sized holes that can accommodate coarse thread or many passes of fine thread. Their uniform shapes create crisp lines when they're worked into a loomed pattern.

Czech beads come in several common sizes, ranging from 18/0 to 6/0. For loom beading, 11/0 and 15/0 are ideal. These beads are shaped like doughnuts and are less uniform than Japanese beads. Their round edges give them a softer look, and they yield a more fluid fabric when they're worked into a loomed piece. The finished piece also has a softer, more sensual feel to it. The holes of these beads are smaller than those in Japanese beads, and their thicker walls make them more durable—and thus more suitable for pieces intended for heavy use.

CHARLOTTE BEADS—These beads, which are Czech-made and have facets cut into them, are a size 13.

TRI-CUT BEADS AND CYLINDER BEADS—Tri-cuts are 11/0 seed beads with random facets that make them sparkle. Shaped as their names imply, cylinder

beads produce very sharp, uniform lines when they're included in loomed beadwork, so they lend themselves to complex designs. Their effect is very nice, but it does lack the sense of fluid movement that the other seed beads offer. The holes in these beads are large enough to take heavier threads. They're fragile, but the crispness of the designs they yield often makes the risk of using these delicate beads worthwhile. What the weak walls of cylinder beads lack in durability is more than compensated for when a delicate design is desired.

tip: The beads in a single hank or tube can vary by as much as two sizes, and some of the beads will be distorted, as well. Removing the worthless beads is called "culling." You can cull as you work, but it's best to take a few minutes to cull out the worst beads before you begin weaving. Pour the beads onto your work surface, and use a paintbrush as a broom to sweep the good beads to one side. Bad beads can be swept away from the good or picked up by stabbing their holes with the brush bristles and lifting them out.

Loop clasps fastened with beads.

To blend bead colors, start weaving with one shade, and add increasing amounts of the second shade as your work progresses.

Other Types of Beads—and Buttons

Any bead that isn't a seed bead—whether it's glass, crystal, stone, or wood—can be useful for embellishment or for making beaded clasps. Buttons also work well for these purposes.

Special Color Techniques

Following are a couple of techniques for handling special bead-color situations.

GRADIENTS—Bead colors from different tubes or hanks don't always match exactly, even if the tubes are from the same lot. To compensate for these variations or to add a little more interest to a beaded background color, you can run a mix of two different shades. As I wove the lariat shown at the top right, I mixed two different shades of green by adding gradually increasing

amounts of the second shade until it eventually replaced the first.

CONFETTI PATTERN—To create a confetti pattern, just mix different colors of beads in a bowl and work them into your piece randomly.

Confetti pattern

I n loom work more than in any other beading technique, your choice of thread is important because the thread will show in your work. Both the weft and the *edge-warp threads* (those along the edges of a piece, where one row of beads ends and another begins) will show along the sides of a piece unless an edging (see page 33) is added, and the inner warps will show slightly between the rows and beads. You should give your thread selections as much consideration as you give to your choice of beads.

Selecting Threads

Depending on the requirements of the piece you plan to make, you'll need to think carefully about the project itself before selecting the types of warp and weft threads to use. Following are descriptions of some things to consider.

The warp threads form the framework for the beads and the weft threads. Ideally, they should be heavier than the weft threads so that they create a good sturdy structure for the "fabric" of the beadwork. You can use the same weight and type of thread for both warp and weft, but do keep in mind that the weft thread should be fine enough to pass through your beads several times; using heavy threads for the weft can make this difficult.

A fine warp thread will yield a silkier feel and more fluid movement to the finished piece; the heavier the threads, the more body the fabric formed with the beadwork will have. In some pieces, the warp threads also function as the finishing and will bear quite a bit of weight, so they should be heavy enough to stand up to wear and to support the weight of the beads.

Because heavier threads aren't as well camouflaged as finer ones, they may be quite visible in your finished work, although in some projects they'll be somewhat hidden beneath the beadwork, or woven in. You may want to use contrasting warp- and weft-thread colors for visual effect.

Types of Thread

The most popular choice of thread for loom work is beading thread, but many alternatives are available, especially for the warps.

Cotton, silk, polyester, and even yarns and cording can be used for different effects. The choices today are many and truly remarkable, so we'll cover only a few of them here.

NYMO AND SILAMIDE BEADING THREADS—These two types of thread are made up of fiber strands, and are both good choices for the weft and the warps for smaller beads. Both move easily and smoothly through the beads' holes and are the staples of any beader's supply arsenal. Both should be pre-stretched before use. Doing this untwists their strands a little, which weakens them, so work in fairly short lengths—an arm-span's length is just about right. Nymo comes in very fine sizes for the finest seed beads. Use the size best suited to your beads.

tip:

Eventually, even if they've been pre-stretched, most beading threads will sometimes stretch when you don't want them to. This isn't a tragedy, but having to patch in a new thread in order to tighten up your work can be very irritating. To tighten up any stretched areas, weave a new thread through the beads, several rows before the distortion, tightening up the rows as you work, and working several rows past the distortion. If any of the stretched threads stick out of the work, gently pull them out as far as you can with a darning needle, trim them close, and then secure them in place either by burning the ends or by using fray prevention liquid (see page 19).

QUILTING THREAD—I prefer a quilting thread for my warp threads, for one simple reason—it doesn't stretch. Cotton or polyester quilting threads, which come in many colors and are usually dyed for the current season's color schemes, are perfect for the warps for size 11/0 beads.

MACHINE-EMBROIDERY THREAD—This thread is intriguing because of its silky feel and lush colors. It's very weak and breaks easily, but it's good for small projects, such as earrings and appliqué patches.

PEARL COTTON THREAD—Excellent for warps, this thread gives an almost corduroy-like effect to finished beadwork.

SILK THREAD—A wonderful thread just for the feel of it as you work, silk can be used for both warp and weft when using Japanese size 11/0 beads. The fabric produced has a very appealing, smooth movement that can't be achieved with any other thread. Do keep in mind that you must glue any knots made in silk; the fibers are so slick they can sometimes unknot themselves.

SEWING THREAD—Many projects require sewing the beadwork onto a fabric or leather surface. Beading threads aren't strong enough for this purpose. Any cotton or polyester sewing thread will work, but buy the more expensive brands. Inexpensive threads are usually poor quality, and the aggravation of working with them isn't worth the few pennies you'd save.

Yarns and Other Fibers

Unlike many other bead stitches, loom work provides an opportunity to incorporate yarns and other fibers by using them as warp threads. Cotton, embroidery, and crochet threads, as well as cords, leather lacing, and wire, can all be used for different effects.

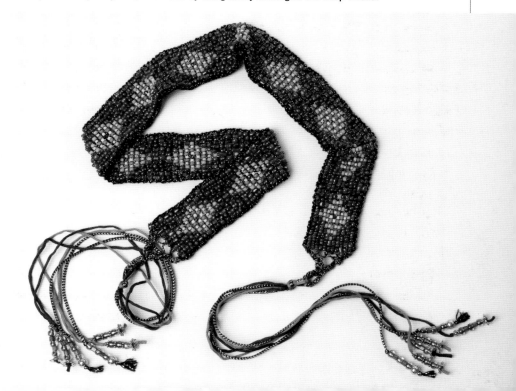

This belt, created by Lucy Elle, was made by using heavy cording as the warp thread.

Wax and Thread Conditioners

Applying wax or other conditioners to thread is sometimes necessary to strengthen thread that will be stressed by passing it through the beads many times, to prevent accidental knotting, and to provide a subtle "glue" that will hold the thread in place. Conditioners can be waxy or oily, so test your conditioned thread on a scrap of fabric before sewing it into a project. If it marks the fabric, don't use it. Also avoid using conditioned threads when you sew fine fabrics or leather. Some commercial conditioners work better than others; you'll want to experiment a bit. I sometimes use an all-natural, wax-based cuticle conditioner instead.

To apply a conditioner, hold it in one hand and use the thumb of that hand to press the thread into its surface. With the other hand, pull the thread through. Repeat a few times, until the thread is evenly coated. Then pinch the thread between your thumb and index finger, and pull it through them a few times to massage the conditioner into the fibers and remove any excess. If you're using wax, the friction will warm it up so it melts and coats the thread evenly.

Beeswax

Beeswax is the most popular conditioner—and a good one—but sometimes it's too hard to apply easily, especially on cold days, and can actually stress the thread. To solve this problem, condition the wax first, using the recipe that follows.

What You Need

- ½ block of beeswax
- Glass or ceramic cup
- Microwave oven
- 2 teaspoons to 1 tablespoon of mineral, olive, or peanut oil. (Don't use vegetable oil; it goes rancid.)
- Optional: several drops of scented oil (mint, cinnamon, orange, or rose, for example)
- Toothpick
- Small paper cup

Break up the half-block of beeswax, place it in the glass or ceramic cup, and microwave on medium for 30 seconds at a time until the wax melts. Carefully add the oils, stirring them in with the toothpick, and pour the mixture into the paper cup. Allow the mixture to cool, then peel away the paper cup.

NEEDLES AND PINS

Most of the time, I prefer to use sharp needles, straight out of a new package; they just feel right to me. On some projects, where the threads will be pulled to shape the piece, however, you'll want to use blunt needles instead, to make sure that the needle doesn't pierce any threads. Many people simply file the needle point down with a nail file, but I find that it's more effective to cut it back with a pair of wire cutters first. Next, I quickly round the blunted point with the roughest surface of a nail file or an emery board that has three grades of grit, for shaping, buffing, and polishing nails. (Shape the point of the needle quickly, just enough to round it; too much filing will add a new point.) Then I smooth out the end of the needle with the buffing surface, and use the finest surface to add a polish.

Beaded needle case (here and at right)

Selecting Needles and Pins

Following are descriptions of the needles and pins you're most likely to need.

#10, #12, #12 SHARPS, AND #15 NEEDLES—You'll use the #10s and #12s for beading, the #12 sharps for embellishing fabrics and sewing, and the #15s for charlottes. For sewing tasks, any sewing needle will do, as long as its eye is larger than your thread, but not so large that the hole it makes as it passes through the fabric is noticeable. For beading, use the largest needle that will fit easily through the beads, for several passes of thread.

#9 BEADING NEEDLE OR SMALL DARNING NEEDLE—These are extremely useful for weaving warp threads (see page 28). Their large holes make repetitive threading easier and make it easier to separate the wefts as you work. They're also good for weaving the weft when using the heavier silk thread and Japanese beads.

STRAIGHT PINS—Useful for holding fabric in place, these can also be run—cautiously—over the warp threads to hold them down. Be careful when using this technique on nymo or silamide threads; they can stretch out of shape.

CORSAGE PINS—These long pins with pearl heads are especially nice for pinning, since their heads are large and don't bury themselves down in the fabric.

In this section, you'll find descriptions of many of the tools that experienced bead-looming artists use.

Selecting Tools

If you're new to loom weaving, you certainly don't have to rush out and buy every tool described here. You'll need a loom, of course, but each project in this book includes a list of the other items required in order to make it, so equip your studio on an as-needed basis.

PIN AWL—This is very handy for separating threads and picking out stitches. A large darning needle makes a good substitute if you can't find an awl that's fine-tipped enough.

CRAFT KNIFE—The replaceable blades of a craft knife will cut a variety of materials into an assortment of shapes.

ROTARY CUTTER, CUTTING MAT, AND A CLEAR ACRYLIC RULER—The rotary cutter is very familiar to quilters and seamstresses. Its round blade works like a pizza cutter. If you're not familiar with this tool, ask for help at your local fabric store. It isn't difficult to use, but can be very dangerous if used incorrectly. Its rolling blade

is particularly sharp, so keep your fingers away from it as you work, and always cover it when the cutter isn't in use. Cutting mats specifically designed for use with rotary cutters are handy for measuring as you cut; they have grids marked on them in 1-inch (2.5 cm) increments. The clear acrylic rulers that are sold with cutting mats are excellent for all projects that require cutting. They come in many shapes and sizes, and are marked with many different combinations of measurements ideal for craft projects. To use one of these rulers as a cutting guide, simply line up the edge of the material to be cut with the appropriate line on the ruler, and hold the ruler in place.

SCISSORS—A variety of scissors is essential for the different projects you can make with loom work. Large scissors are useful for cutting fabrics, leather, and backing materials. Small embroidery scissors are invaluable for trimming threads and trimming in close spaces.

WIRE CUTTERS AND EMERY BOARDS—These come in handy for blunting sharp needles.

BEANBAGS—Small beanbags are great for weighing down and securing glued pieces as the glue dries. To make your own, just take a look at the Tip that follows.

tip:

To make a beanbag, cut two matching fabric squares or rectangles, any size you wish. Sew the pieces together around the edges, leaving an opening just large enough to turn the bag inside out. Turn the sewn pieces inside out so the seams are on the interior. Fill the bag with rice, beans, sand, or kitty litter. Fold the edges of the opening down inside the bag, and sew it closed, using a hidden stitch.

LAUNDRY MARKERS—Use these markers, which come in a variety of colors, to camouflage threads that stand out and are distracting along the edge of the warp and along the edges of *terminals* (the finished ends of a piece of loomed beadwork). Odd colors can be matched by combining two or more colors. A blending marker is also handy for adjusting colors that aren't quite right. Always test markers on scraps first. Trying to camouflage something only to have it look even worse is very frustrating; you'll either have to rework it or color the whole thing.

HOLE PUNCH—This tool is excellent for exactly the function you'd think—punching holes. Two types are readily available at many craft and fabric stores: the ever-popular hand punch, which is squeezed to punch the hole; and the newer hydraulic punch, which is operated by holding the punch in place and pushing the handle downward.

OTHER TOOLS—A fabric tape measure, pencil, round-nosed pliers, circle template, and an iron and ironing board will prove useful for some projects.

MATERIALS

As well as beads, many loomed projects incorporate adhesives, armature materials—materials that serve as supports for your beadwork—and closures or findings.

Adhesives for Fabric and Leather

Different adhesives work best on different materials, so make sure you refer to the materials list for your selected project before you purchase any.

FLEXIBLE FABRIC GLUE—Solid-drying glues add an undesirable stiffness to beaded projects and also become brittle over time. Flexible glue, on the other hand, works well with fabrics and backings because it "moves" along with the fabric. It's also ideal for appliquéd loom work.

CONTACT CEMENT—This adhesive works on leather, but it won't adhere to some polyester fabrics such as webbing, so always test it on your fabrics before using it in a project. And keep in mind that contact cement tends to dry to a nasty yellow color; pay special attention when applying it so that it doesn't show in your finished piece.

FUSIBLE WEBBING—Sold under a variety of trade names, this product provides an excellent way to "glue" two pieces of fabric or interfacing together. To use fusible webbing, sandwich it between the two fabrics and iron it in place, following the manufacturer's instructions for times and temperatures.

FRAY PREVENTION LIQUID AND JEWELER'S GLUE—Although jeweler's glue will work on knots and is a better quality than the other instant glues on the market, a fray prevention product is made specifically for fabrics, and I trust its long-term durability more. It makes sense to use an adhesive that's less likely to become brittle over time.

PAINTER'S TAPE OR MASKING TAPE—Either of these tapes can be used to stabilize beadwork on a surface as you work. Painter's tape works well on sensitive materials such as leather since it sticks without bonding to the surfaces. Be careful with masking tape; it sometimes adheres so well that it lifts felt and leather surfaces. In a pinch, masking tape can also be used for taped terminals (see page 28).

TWO-SIDED TAPE—With adhesive on both of its surfaces, this tape offers a quick and easy way to secure two layers of material together in order to stabilize them long enough to stitch them down.

CLOTH MEDICAL TAPE—The adhesive on medical tape is designed not to irritate skin and is much gentler than the adhesive on masking tape. In addition, because cloth medical tape stays much more flexible over the long run, it's the ideal tape to use for taped terminals (see page 28).

Armature Materials

Many of the projects in this book consist of loomed beadwork that is attached to a fabric or leather armature, which serves as the beadwork's foundation. An armature often helps to define and support the function of a piece, even when it isn't readily visible; think of it as the "skeleton" of a finished piece. Armatures can be made with the many materials listed in this section or can be purchased items such as jackets, dog leashes, guitar straps, belts, and visors.

FELT—Whenever possible, I prefer to use wool felt rather than acrylic felt. My preference is purely sensory; wool felt feels softer and has a smoother surface than acrylic felt, which is coarse and a little thicker. Both can be cut easily with scissors or a rotary cutter.

SYNTHETIC SUEDE—A polyester substitute for leather, synthetic suede is very thin but has a leathery quality. Although it's relatively expensive, it's well worth the cost and is an excellent product for those of us who dislike using animal hides. It's much easier to sew by hand than leather and is very easy to cut.

LEATHER—Although leathers come in many different grades and from different animals, the most popular are cowhide and *buckskin* (deer hide). Cowhide is usually thicker than buckskin. Even though buckskin is a little like silk (it likes to move around and stretch in odd ways as you work with it), it's the best leather to use for most projects.

Craft-quality hides are fine for many projects, but they do have flaws in their surfaces and vary in thickness, so pay attention when you cut them.

To cut leather with a rotary cutter, you must stabilize it first. Lay out a piece that is larger than the piece required for your project, and smooth the surface, stretching it out flat but not taut. Tape the edges with painter's tape. Then cut one good, straight edge, using a ruler and rotary cutter. Next, lift up the ruler without disturbing the leather, and gently reposition it for the next cut.

tip:

You can hand-sew leather in much the same way as you do fabric, but don't try to pass the needle through its entire thickness. When you're sewing two leather edges together, for example, either pass the needle through the inner edges of the surfaces that are touching, or through each outer edge.

INTERFACING—This stiff fabric is similar to a mixture of cardstock and felt. It stiffens and supports finer fabrics, making them easier to shape and improving their function. Interfacing ranges from very thin to thick; choose a thickness to accommodate your project.

CARDSTOCK—This heavy paper, typically used to make cards, is very useful in some projects. It serves the same function as interfacing, but bends without creasing.

PADDING—For many projects, padding the beadwork itself is useful. This can be done with a strip of felt, batting, or even bias tape—anything that will serve as a support and as padding between the beadwork and the armature. Cut the padding slightly smaller than the beadwork, and baste it onto the armature fabric just to tack it down in place. Sew the loom work down over the top.

CHIPBOARD OR MAT BOARD—These heavy-duty poster boards, commonly used in framing, can serve as a subsurface armature to give a project its shape. Cut the board with a craft knife and ruler, making several passes with a sharp blade. The board is too thick to cut in a single pass, no matter how hard you press with the knife; using too much pressure on the blade just increases the risk of slips that can cause severe cuts. Relax, use a steady but gentle hand, and make several passes.

FOAM BOARD—This is a sheet of foam that's sandwiched between two sheets of poster board. As with mat board, you must make more than one pass in order to cut it. Use a ruler and craft knife to make your first cut through the top layer of poster board. With the second pass, score the foam. On the third pass, cut the poster board on the back.

WEBBING—These flat, woven-fiber straps can be purchased in different widths and a limited number of colors. They're useful for making belts, dog leashes and collars, and guitar straps.

Findings and Closures

Many projects in this book call for *findings*—separate components such as belt buckles, earring wires, jewelry clasps, 'D' rings, hooks, and closures. Findings define the function of a piece—as a necklace, bracelet, or leash, for example. You can make or purchase them, but always try to balance their form and function. It doesn't matter how beautiful findings are if they don't function correctly for the pieces to which they're attached.

The projects in this book list the findings you'll need, and you'll find general instructions for attaching them on page 31.

The first step of weaving on a loom is stringing the warp threads—a process known as "warping the loom." The warp threads, which are suspended across the loom's length, are the heart of your loomed work; they hold it all together and establish the skeleton or foundation for your beadwork. The spaces between them serve as "parking places" for the beads in each row. You'll need one more warp thread than the number of beads to be used for the color pattern in one row. For example, if your work will be nine beads wide, you'll need 10 warp threads.

Warped sleigh loom

Warping a Sleigh Loom

Choose a loom 8 to 12 inches (20.3 to 30.5 cm) longer than the desired length of the finished beadwork. Begin by attaching one end of the thread on a bobbin or spool to an anchor on the loom. Pulling the thread off the bobbin as you work, bring it up over the bridge, across the length of the loom, and over the second bridge. Hook the thread onto the anchor at this end.

Next, bring the thread back over the bridge and hook it to the anchor on the opposite end. Continue to work back and forth across the bridges, spacing the thread lengths evenly as you work by positioning them across the spacers. Keep the thread tension even and snug; warp threads with sufficient tension on them will help ensure that your weft threads will be taut.

tip: To add strength to projects that will see heavy use, it's a good idea to double the edge warps (the outermost warp threads) by adding an extra thread to each one. As you add rows of beads, you'll work each set of doubled threads as one. When you work the terminals of a piece, you'll weave the ends of these doubled edge-warp threads into your beadwork in a different way than the other warp threads (see page 28).

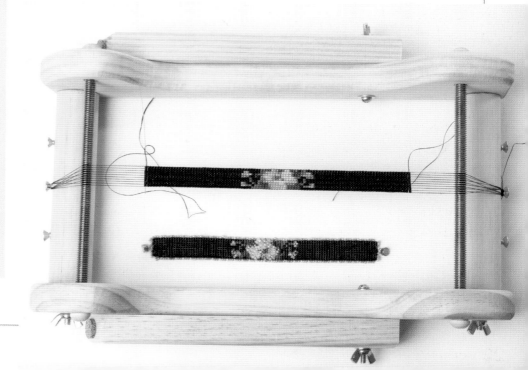

figure 1

Warping a Roller Loom

In order to finish off the terminals of completed loom-worked straps, you need at least 6 inches (15.2 cm) of extra length at each end of the warp threads, so start by cutting individual warp threads that are 18 inches (45.7 cm) longer than the length of your finished project. (Remember to cut one more thread than there are beads in the widest row.)

Knot one end of the group of cut threads, and attach the knot to the anchor on the roller at one end of the loom. Using a comb to keep the threads untangled and separated, roll almost the entire lengths of the threads up on the roller; then secure the roller to hold them in place.

Knot together the other ends of the threads, and attach the knot to the anchor of the other roller. Secure the roller so the threads are stretched loosely over the bridges. Using an awl or darning needle, separate the threads and position each one in a spacer notch at each end of the loom. Once the threads are neatly organized, tighten them by adjusting the rollers.

WEFT THREADS

The weft thread anchors the beads in rows across the warp threads. Each complete row takes two passes of weft thread to complete.

The Stop Bead

Rather than knotting one end of your weft thread, add a *stop bead*. String a bead onto the thread, and slide it down to about 12 inches (30.5 cm) from the tail. Wrap the thread around the bead by passing the needle back through the bead hole, and pull the thread snug (see figure 1).

The thread tension will hold this stop bead in place, while still allowing you to move it up and down the thread when you want to alter the tension on the beads. After working a few rows to stabilize the beads, you can remove the stop bead at any time, and either weave the thread tail into the work to create a blunt terminal, or use it to weave a pointed terminal when your beadwork is complete. (See Terminals on page 27.)

The First Pass

String all of the beads for the row onto your weft thread. Then, with the weft thread *underneath* the warp threads, push each strung bead up between two warp threads.

The Second Pass

Hold the beads in place between the warp threads while you run your needle back through them, this time with the weft thread *above* the warp threads. Positioning the weft thread first above and then below the warp threads is what holds the beads in place.

tip: Weave the first row of a piece in increments. Position only the first few beads between the warp threads and make the second pass through them (see figure 2). Then

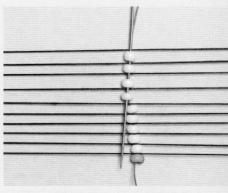

When creating a first row, make the second pass through only a few beads at a time.

position a few more strung beads in that row and continue the second pass through them. Repeat until the row is finished. Once you've loomed the first row and tightened up the thread, the "parking places" between the warp threads will be better aligned, so you'll be able to work whole rows rather than just a few beads at a time.

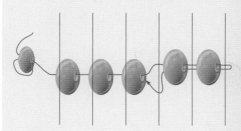

figure 2

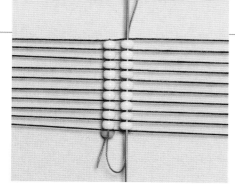

Adding the second row

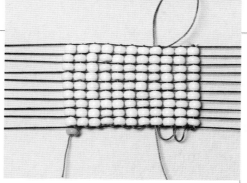

Ending a weft thread

Subsequent Rows

Work each row with two passes of the weft thread—the first with the beads strung and parked in place under the warp threads, and the second with the thread running through the beads and over the warp threads (see figure 3).

Ending Weft Threads

Whether you've run out of thread or are ending a project, you'll need to add new threads to your work. To add a new weft thread, many people simply use a surgeon's knot (see page 40) to attach a new thread to the end of an old one. I find that sooner or later these knots trip me up when they're too large to pass easily through a bead. I much prefer a wrapped ending on a new, anchored thread (see Adding Weft Threads).

There are several steps to ending a weft thread. First, make an *edge wrap* by wrapping the weft thread around the edge warp to move it back a few rows. Now pass the thread back through a row of beads and wrap it around the opposite edge warp. Then pass it back through the same row again (see figure 4). Trim the tail and secure it as necessary. (Add a drop of fray prevention liquid or jeweler's glue if you like.)

To secure nylon or polyester weft

threads, just burn their ends with a lighter. The beads usually insulate the warp threads, so they don't burn as easily as you might think, but do practice before burning threads on an important piece.

Adding Weft Threads

Tie a wrapped knot (see page 40) at the end of a new thread. The larger the hole in the bead, the more times the thread should be wrapped to knot it. To anchor the new thread in place, run it through the last row worked, and pull the knot into the row until it snags on the threads inside one of the bead holes. For extra security, before you begin the next row, tie the weft thread to the edge-warp thread with a half-hitch knot (see figure 5 and page 40).

Removing Beadwork from the Loom

To remove the beadwork, cut the threads close to the loom anchors at one end. Then slide off or cut the threads at the opposite end, and cut any loops that remain at the ends of the warp threads.

To ensure that the rows in your project don't move around and become displaced, secure the ends of the weft by *anchor weaving* them (see page 28).

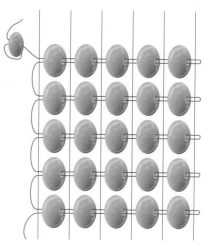

figure 3

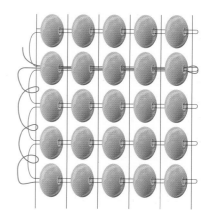

figure 4

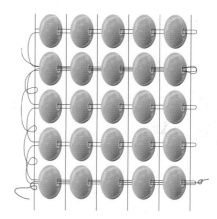

figure 5

The broken-warp technique can create lovely variations along the length of a loomed bracelet.

C hanging the warps that hold the weft together or altering the steps of weaving a weft can create some fun and interesting effects.

Broken Warp

To work a broken warp, you string beads onto each warp thread as you warp the loom. These beads are suspended between the bridges and make strands between the woven sections (see the Broken Warp Necklace on page 56). Adding the same number of beads to each warp thread will produce a beaded strap with a very nice texture. Stringing an increasing or decreasing number of beads on each warp thread will create strands of graduated lengths.

Intersections

Strips of beadwork that intersect with a previously loomed piece and extend outward from it are easy to create on a sleigh loom. The Stellular project on page 94 offers a great example.

First, weave a strip of beadwork to the desired length and width. Remove the piece from the loom, and finish with an appropriate terminal at each end (see Terminals on page 27).

Next, you're going to warp your loom again, incorporating the original loomed piece as you do. Start by threading a needle with as much thread as you can handle easily, and tie one end of the thread to one of the loom anchors. Now pass this needle all the way through a beaded weft row of the

New warp threads, run through the rows of an existing loomed strip, serve as the base for added sections of intersecting beadwork.

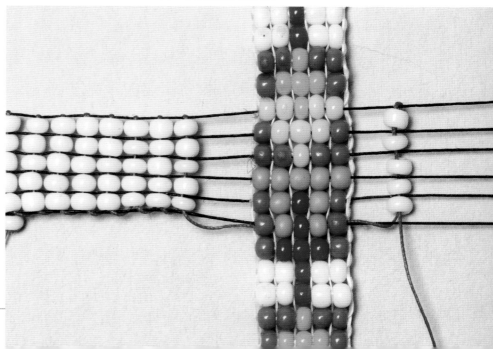

loomed strip, where the intersection that you're going to create will be located. Tie the thread to the anchor on the opposite end of the loom.

Pass the needle back through the next weft row of the beaded strip, and attach it to the opposite anchor. Continue to run the warp thread through beaded rows until you've added as many warps as desired for the intersecting beadwork. If your warp thread becomes too short, just tie it to an anchor, and continue warping with a new thread.

Thread a needle and attach the thread to the strip of beadwork by knotting it and then passing it through a few rows, wrapping it around the edge warps to camouflage it, and exiting where you'd like to start the intersection. Now you're ready to add the intersecting beadwork. Just weave your new weft rows on either side of the first strip.

Cut Warp

Some patterns, such as the one for the Twisted Warp Bracelet on page 46, call for spaces in the woven beadwork. These are created by cutting some of the warp threads while the beadwork is on the loom and weaving their ends back through the rows (see figure 6). To resume the beadwork, string new warp threads to replace the cut ones, as you would when beginning a project, but run them over the top of the existing loom work.

tip: The cut-warp technique can also be used to repair broken warp threads. Weave the broken threads into the work. Attach a new thread to an anchor, and weave it between the appropriate weft threads before attaching it to the other anchor.

Split Warp

Working on only some of the warp threads in a section of a project produces a split warp. The unused warp threads are cut and woven back into the beadwork after the piece has been removed from the loom (see figure 7).

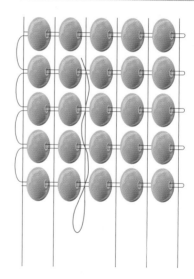

figure 6

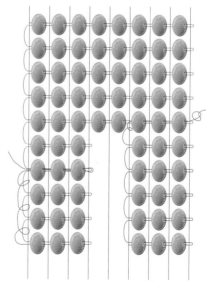

figure 7

A split warp, with beads of different colors on each side

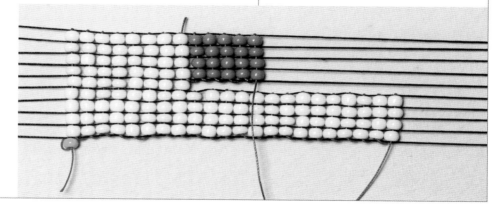

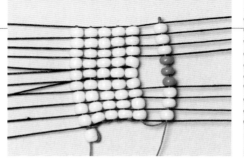
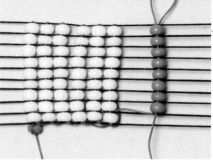

Bridged weft

Decreasing on the left

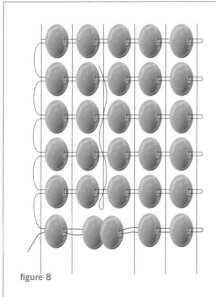

figure 8

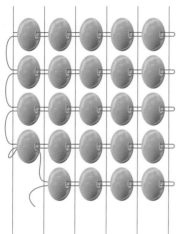

figure 9

Bridged Weft

A bridged weft is a span of beads that doesn't have warp threads passing through it (see figure 8). These beads, which are loose on their weft threads, span an area between two woven sections and are ready for special treatment. In the Aztec Sky light switch cover (see page 90), they hide the screws on the switch cover itself and maintain the color pattern, but because they're movable they allow you to reach the screws when necessary.

Decreasing

Decreasing rows to narrow a point is easier than increasing, so on most projects you'll want to weave the main (widest) portion of the piece first, and then go back to work the ends by decreasing them. Starting with one or just a few beads and increasing the project width as you go is more difficult. (The exceptions to this rule—working some broken-warp projects and working with bead lace—are covered later.) Although you may find it confusing to create the widest area first and then decrease to narrow the ends (this requires working in both directions on the warp threads), you'll improve with practice.

DECREASING ON THE LEFT—Bring the weft thread under and around the edge-

warp thread and back through the first bead in the last row. String on the appropriate number of beads, and weave the new row (see figure 9).

DECREASING ON THE RIGHT—String on the appropriate number of beads and bring them up under the warp threads. Bring the needle up between the warp threads in the appropriate place, and work the second pass of the row (see figure 10).

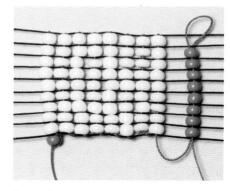

Decreasing on the right

Increasing

Increasing is a little more challenging than decreasing, but is well worth the effort.

INCREASING ON THE LEFT—Take a good look at figure 11 before beginning. Wrap the weft thread around and under the warp thread that the last bead in the last row was worked on. String one or more

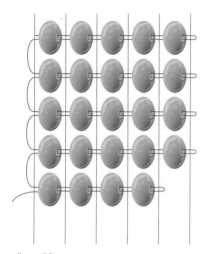

figure 10

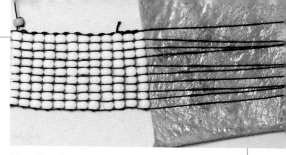

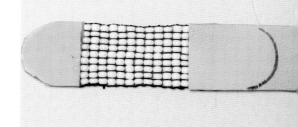

Warp threads arranged on a glue-covered piece of leather

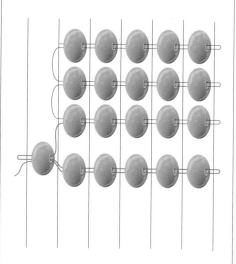

figure 11

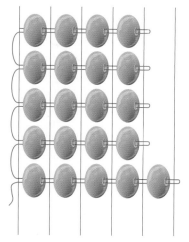

figure 12

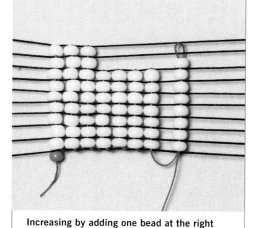

Increasing by adding one bead at the right

beads for the increased row, and bring the thread over the next warp thread to the left. Then string on the appropriate number of beads for the rest of the row, park them in place, and bring the thread up and around the right-hand edge-warp thread before passing back through the whole row. Pull snug to straighten up the row.

INCREASING ON THE RIGHT—String the desired number of beads, and work the row as shown in figure 12.

TERMINALS

The terminals (or ends of a piece of loomed beadwork) can be created in a number of different ways.

Leather Terminals

Cut two matching pieces of leather, each wider than the beadwork and longer than the desired length of the finished terminal. Apply contact cement or flexible glue to the entire inner surface of each piece. Position the warp-thread ends on the glue-covered surface of one piece of leather, with the beads lined up against one edge. Sandwich the second piece of leather over the first. Allow the glue to dry, then cut the leather to shape.

The leather terminal on the left has been trimmed to shape; the one at the right is marked for cutting.

TOMBSTONE-SHAPED TERMINAL— First trim the sandwiched leather pieces to the width of the strap. Then, using a circle template, draw a line to establish the rounded shape of the terminal, and cut along that line.

tip:

A *netted terminal* (instructions are provided on page 29) will add some extra "tooth" for the glue-covered leather to grip.

BAIL (KEY-RING) TERMINAL—Work a netted terminal (see page 29) and cut it short. Cut an hourglass shape out of leather that's been folded over. Unfold the leather, position the key ring in its center, and arrange the terminal on one half of it. Apply glue to the two end areas of the

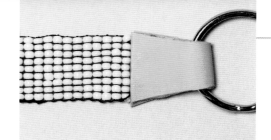

Netted terminal arranged on leather, with a key ring in place

leather piece, and fold the leather over so the glue-covered areas meet, lining up the doubled leather edges with the last row of the beadwork.

Taped Terminals

Lay the beadwork down on a work surface. If you like, before you create the taped terminal, use the warp threads to make slide knots (see page 40) along the edge of the beadwork. Smooth and straighten the warp threads so they're even and neat. Cut a piece of cloth tape a little more than twice the width of the beadwork. Center it sticky side down over the warp threads, with one edge lined up along the edge of the beadwork or the slide knots, and press it down in place. Lift up the beadwork, with the tape attached, and turn it over. Fold the edges of the tape over toward the center. Burnish the tape with scissor handles or the smooth back of the awl.

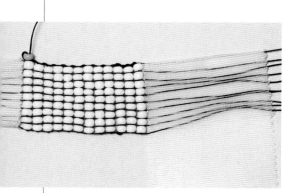

Tape placed over the neatly arranged warp threads

Woven Terminals

Weaving on the warp threads not only anchors them but can also provide attractive terminals for many loomed pieces.

Thread woven terminal

ANCHOR WEAVE—Threading each of the edge-warp threads across one another through the last row of beads will anchor or secure the end of your beadwork, so there's a minimum of movement as you finish the rest of the warp threads. (Note that anchoring these threads isn't necessary when you plan to create taped or leather terminals.)

Thread the first edge-warp thread onto a needle, pass it through the last row of beadwork, and trim it. Weave the other edge-warp thread in the same fashion, in the opposite direction. If the holes in the beads are too small for the second thread, wrap that thread around the edge warp and weave into the second or third row.

If you're working with doubled edge-warp threads, you probably won't be able to anchor them all in the same row; beads will only accept a few passes of thread through their holes. Instead, anchor weave

only one thread from each double set. Then work each of the extra two warp threads back several rows by wrapping it around the edge warp and then weaving it into the beadwork (see figure 13).

tip:

When weaving warp threads, you'll occasionally run into a bead that's been so filled with thread you can't pass the needle through it. When this happens, jump a bead by passing your needle between the weft threads and up to the next row. Forcing a needle through a bead can break it. If this happens, you'll have to remove the row and patch a new thread in (see page 23) several rows before, weave the row again, and weave the thread through a few rows after the replacement row (figure 14).

WARP WEAVE—Once the anchor weave has been completed and secures the rows in place, weave each of the remaining warp threads back up into the work between the beads in a series of rows. One by one, thread each warp thread onto a needle.

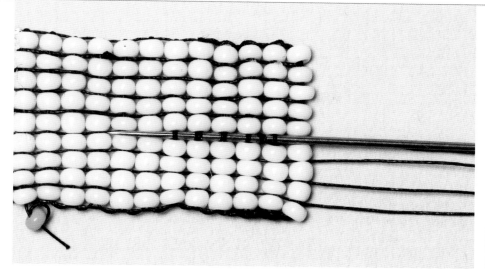

Warp weaving secures the ends of the warp threads.

Skipping the very last row of beads (if you include it, you'll just "un-warp" your warp thread), push the needle *between* the two passes of weft thread that run through each row of beads, continuing on up between the beads in several rows (see figure 15).

tip:

Warp-weave with a #9 beading needle or a small darning needle. These needles are much easier to thread than other types, so your work will go much faster. Because you've already secured your rows with the anchor weave, these needles won't distort the bead placement at all.

THREAD-WOVEN TERMINAL—With the beadwork still on the loom, weave the weft thread through the warp threads in an under/over fashion to create ¹/₄ to ¹/₂ inch (6 mm to 1.3 cm) of woven thread (see figure 16). Using a paintbrush, saturate the top and bottom surfaces of the woven area with flexible fabric glue. Clean any glue from the beads with a damp rag. When the glue has dried, remove the work from the loom.

KNOTTED AND NETTED TERMINALS— To create a knotted terminal, you'll make slide knots (see page 40) along the last row of beadwork. Using an awl, pin, or needle, tie two warp threads together, and slide the knot close to the last row of beadwork; don't make the knot too tight. Double up threads when you have an odd number.

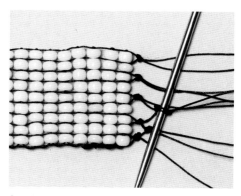

Creating a netted terminal

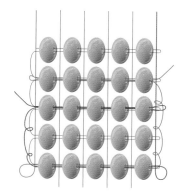

figure 13

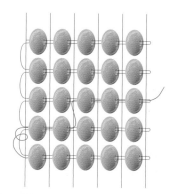

figure 14

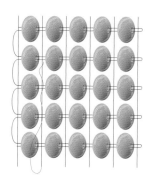

figure 15

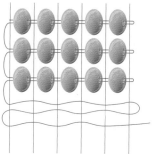

figure 16

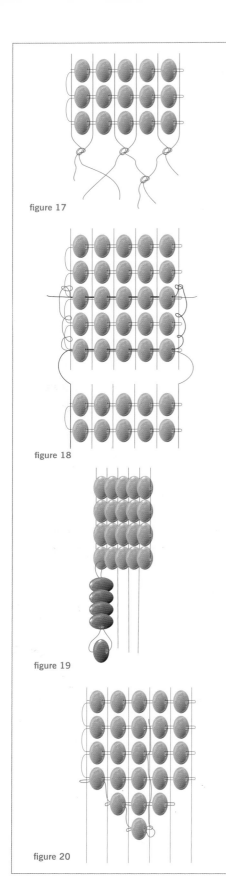

figure 17

figure 18

figure 19

figure 20

To work a netted terminal, tie rows of knots to form a net (see figure 17). Alternate rows will leave the first and last warp threads loose; just tie these free threads into subsequent rows. Space the consecutive rows of knots evenly; altering the space between knots will alter the appearance of the netting.

CONNECTION-WEAVE TERMINAL—To join two pieces of loomed work end-to-end and to simultaneously anchor the rows, anchor weave the edge-warp threads at the end of one piece into a row of beads in the other piece (see figure 18). Repeat to anchor-weave the edge-warp threads of the other piece, and then warp-weave the remaining threads.

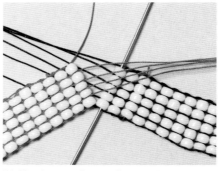

Working the warp threads of one end into the other

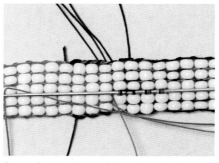

Connecting two pieces of loomed work end-to-end

FRINGED TERMINAL—After removing the beadwork from the loom, create a fringe by stringing beads onto the warp threads before weaving them into the weft (figure 19). You'll need to plan ahead, as your warp threads must be long enough to accommodate the fringe beads. (For full instructions on fringe techniques, see page 37.)

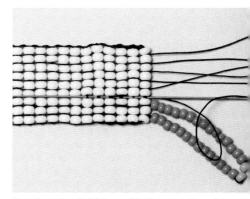

Creating a beaded fringe with the warp threads

POINTED TERMINAL—Decrease each row by two beads (see page 26) until the rows are three, five, or seven beads in width (see figure 20). Weave the warps to finish, or add a clasp (see page 31).

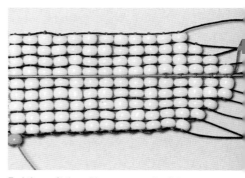

End the weft thread by warp weaving into the bead work.

In this section, you'll find instructions for creating a variety of woven closures and for attaching purchased findings.

Making Bead and Button Closures

A number of different closures can be created with beads, buttons, and thread. Following are just a few.

STRAP CATCH—Weave a section three to seven beads wide, and long enough to wrap around a hook bead or button at the end of a terminal. Fold this narrow strip back toward the beadwork, and warp-weave the threads into the beadwork.

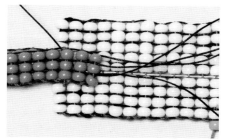

A folded strap catch in progress

tip:

The tension of the warp threads that you've woven through the weft threads will make the strap catch secure enough for regular use. If you worry that the warp threads might pull out of a project, weave their ends as you would the ends of weft threads, through the rows.

BEADED HOOK AND CATCH—Warp-weave all but the two innermost warp threads. To create a hook, first string a few beads in a fringe-like fashion (see page 37) onto one of the remaining warp threads, ending with a large bead or button and a stop bead. Then run the thread back through all the beads except for the last one strung, and warp-weave it into the beadwork (see figure 21). Use the second warp thread to reinforce this hook by running it down and back up through the strung beads, and warp weaving it, as well.

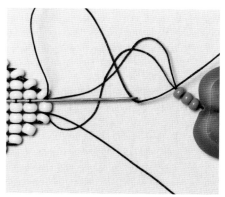

Working a clasp bead

Weave the catch at the other end of the piece by stringing enough beads to make a loop that fits easily around the hook bead. Warp-weave the end of this thread into the beadwork. Use the second warp thread to reinforce the loop.

BUTTONHOLE CATCH—Start by weaving a strap bracelet, making it approximately 1½ inches (3.8 cm) shorter than the desired length for the finished bracelet.

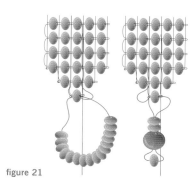

figure 21

Then split the warp (see page 25), and on one side work a strip that is one row longer than the diameter of the bead or button to be used and half the width of the bracelet. On the other side, weave a strip with rows one bead shorter than half the width of the bracelet.

Reconnect the split by working the full width of the warps. You'll be left with a buttonhole. Work a terminal at that end. At the other end, use the two innermost warp threads to attach the bead or button. (See the Beaded Hook and Catch instructions [above].)

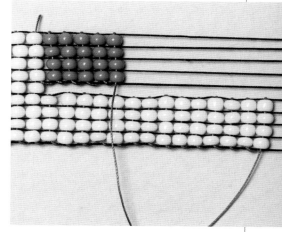

Making a buttonhole clasp by splitting the warp

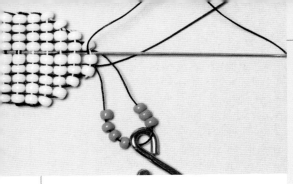

When attaching a clasp to the warp threads, you may want to add a few beads for their decorative effect.

Attaching Metal Findings

Some of the projects in this book include specific instructions for attaching findings; for others, simply follow the general attachment instructions in this section.

CLASPS—Warp-weave all but the two innermost warp threads. Use one of these threads to work a loop that incorporates the bail of the first half of the clasp, and finish off by weaving this thread into the beadwork (see figure 22). Use the second thread to tighten up and reinforce the loop, and finish off in the same way. Work the second half of the clasp in the same fashion.

JUMP RINGS—These small wire rings link one part of the project to a finding. Open the jump ring, slip on the finding, close the ring, and then attach the ring to the beadwork with a small beaded loop, just as you would a clasp. (Make sure you've

figure 22

tip:

To avoid distorting a jump ring when you open it, pull its ends apart sideways. If you enlarge the ring by pulling the tips of the ends directly away from each other, you'll have a hard time getting them to meet again when you try to close the ring.

closed the jump ring tightly, or your thread may slip out of the opening.)

SPLIT RINGS—Like jump rings, split rings, which look like miniature key rings, serve as links between projects and findings, and are attached with small loops. Open up the slit in the ring, slide the bail of the finding over one end of the ring, and slide it into place.

BARRETTES—These inexpensive findings tend to be flimsy, but I actually prefer them because they hold better in fine hair than French clips do. For thick, heavy hair, use French clips.

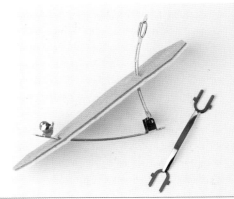

FRENCH CLIPS—Unlike the other hair clips, French clips can't be taken apart. Cut the slits in the armature, open the slits, slide the French clip into the slits, and glue it in place.

BEAD TIPS—With the thread coming off the loom work, string the desired number of beads and one bead tip, with the loop of the bead tip facing away from the end of the loom work. Tie a wrapped slide knot on the end of the thread, making sure that it's large enough not to pull through the bead tip. Trim the tail, and add a drop of glue or fray prevention liquid to the knot. Use round-nosed pliers to bend the loop over and in place.

CLAMSHELL BEAD TIPS—These are worked in the same fashion as bead tips, except that you must close the shell after securing the knot.

tip:

Making a slide knot takes a bit of practice! Kinking your beads or slipping even slightly with your pin or awl will leave a gap between the tip and the beads on the finished piece. Before you remove your knotting tool, double-check the spacing of your beads.

Bullet end, with its wire end looped through a knot

WIRED BULLET (OR CONE) ENDS—

String a number of beads onto each warp thread. Tie the ends of your strands into a loose knot that's close to the beads. Slide the end of the bullet wire through the center of the knot so that the tip extends beyond it. Add fray prevention liquid to the center of the knot, around the stem of the wire, and tighten the knot up around the wire. Bring the tip of the wire back around the knot, and wrap it around the wire stem. Run the opposite end of the wire up through a bullet end. Using round-nosed pliers, form a loop or a wrapped loop in the wire, and trim it. Attach a clasp or link to the other end of the beadwork.

GROMMETS—

Punch a hole through the fabric or leather. Push the grommet through the hole, making sure that its front is at the front of the project. Use the punch to crimp the back edges of the grommet onto the fabric.

BUCKLES, 'D' RINGS, KEY RINGS, AND SWIVEL SNAPS—

Fold over and stitch the end of the ribbon fabric or webbing, so its raw edges are tucked inside and hidden. Push the sewn end through the bar or ring bail of the finding, and fold it over the bail. Arrange the fabric or webbing neatly in place, with its edges aligned, and sew it in place.

EDGINGS

An edging consists of beads added along the length of the edge-warp threads. When worked well, it complements the color pattern of the beadwork and adds a little extra pizzazz.

Picot Edgings

A picot consists of a few beads or threads that loop out from the beaded work to give the piece a lacy look. To work a picot edging, you'll use a hook stitch to attach the beads to the edge-warp thread.

ONE-BEAD PICOT—Begin with your thread exiting the last bead in a row of the beaded strap. String on three beads, then pass the thread under the edge-warp thread and up through the last bead of the three just added. Pull the thread snug so the beads rest side by side (see figure 23).

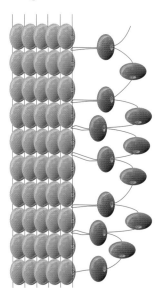

figure 23

Each subsequent set of picot beading will "borrow" the last bead of the set preceding it. String on two beads, then pass the thread under the edge-warp thread and up through the last bead of the two just added. Pull the thread snug again.

Working the picot edging at the end of every row will pull on the edge-warp thread and cause the rows to buckle. To avoid this, change the spacing by skipping a row every third stitch.

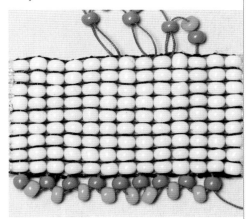

One-bead picot edging

TWO-STEP PICOT EDGING—With the thread coming out of a bead, string on four beads. Run the thread under the edge-warp thread one row ahead and back through the last bead added. Pull tight.

*Now string one bead. Run the thread under the edge-warp thread at the next row and back through the bead just added. Pull tight. Add three beads, run through the edge-warp thread two rows ahead, and back through the bead just added (see figure 24).

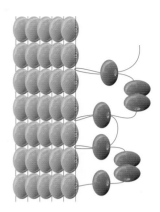

figure 24

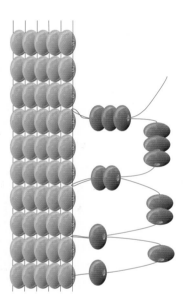

figure 25

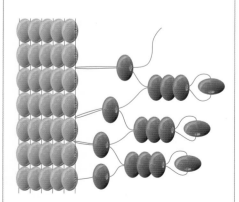

figure 26

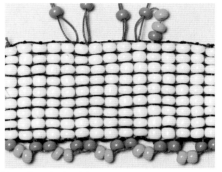

Two-step picot edging

For subsequent sets, repeat from * along the edge of the beadwork.

After the last set of four beads have been worked, end by running the thread tail into the loom work (see figure 24).

MULTI-DROP PICOT EDGING—You can change the look of your edging by altering the numbers and types of beads used to make the legs (the sets of beads that rise perpendicularly from the edge of a loomed piece) and rungs (the beads that span the legs), and by changing the gaps between the bridges

Multi-drop picot edging

(the threads between two beads). There is no "rule" to this alteration; different numbers of beads will produce different effects (see figure 25). Some pattern graphs will specify how many of what type of bead to use.

EDGE FRINGE—This fringe is a cross between the one-bead picot and the two-legged fringe (see page 38). Between each of the "hooked" picot beads, just add a short two-legged fringe (see figure 26).

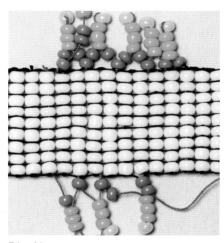

Edge fringe

Brick-Stitched Points

Start with your thread running out of a bead of the loom work, and work a picot edging up to where you'd like to make your point.

The last bead in the last set of the picot edging will be the first bead of the brick-stitched point. String on the second bead, run the thread under the next bridge and back up through the bead just added. Pull tight. Repeat this until you have the number of beads required for the first row, or base, of your point.

To begin the next row of the point, first take a close look at the photos. String on two beads, and pass the needle under the second bridge and back up through the second bead added. Work the brick stitch until you have used all the bridges.

Begin a new row. Each row that you work will decrease by one bead.

When you finish the row that has only two beads, it's time to add a point bead

(see figure 27). String on one bead, run the needle down through the last brick-stitched bead and through one bead in each brick-stitched row, all the way down to the second-to-last bead of the first row and up through the last bead in the first row. Your thread is now ready and in place for you to begin your picot edging again. Count the last bead of the first row of brick stitch as the first bead of the picot edging.

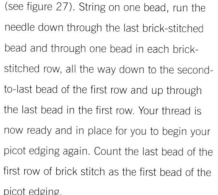

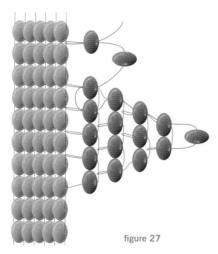

figure 27

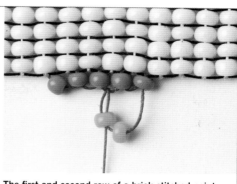

The first and second row of a brick-stitched point

Last two-bead row of a brick-stitched point

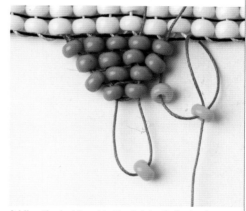

Adding the last bead to the brick-stitched point before continuing the picot edging

Brick-stitched points in different sizes

tip:

When working the brick stitch, pass through the first two beads of the row twice to tighten and straighten them up.

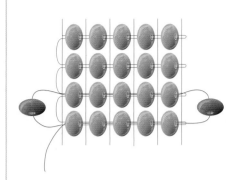

figure 28

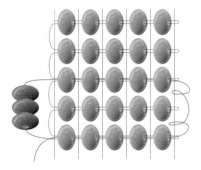

figure 29

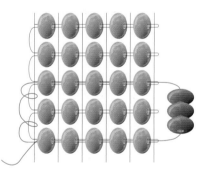

figure 30

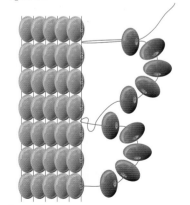

figure 31

Weft Edging

An edging can be added as the weft is worked by stringing on one or more additional beads before running the thread back through the beadwork rows. Each of the weft-edging graphs in this book shows a thread path for adding the beads, which rows to pass through, and where to wrap the thread around the edge-warp thread.

To add a single-bead edge weft on either side, string on the bead, and then pass through the previous row and back through the working row (see figure 28).

To add three beads to the left, string on three beads and pass through the third row back. Edge wrap along the right-hand edge, back to the working row. Pass through the working row and begin weaving again (see figure 29).

To add three beads on the right, edge wrap back three rows and pass through the row. String on three beads and pass through the working row (see figure 30). Begin weaving again.

Old-Fashioned Whip Edging

A whip edging is worked as a beaded half-hitch (see page 40). With the thread exiting the beadwork, begin by stringing three to seven beads. Pass the thread under the edge-warp thread, two to six spaces away. Bring the needle through the loop and pull tight (see figure 31). Repeat along the edge warp, keeping the stitches evenly spaced.

Old-fashioned whip edging

Rolled Edge

A rolled edge is more or less a beaded whipstitch (see page 41) that covers the wide edge of a piece. Begin by anchoring a knot in the fabric of the armature and exiting close to the edge of the fabric. String on an odd number of beads—one more than is needed for the thickness of the fabric layers. Pass the thread through the layers of fabric and along the inside of the edge-warp thread (see figure 32). Bring the beads up tight. Repeat along the whole edge. Crowd the stitches at any corners by stitching through the fabric three times, placing these stitches side by side.

Working a rolled edge

Making a needle-tatted edge with halfhitch knots

Needle-Tatted Edge

Work half-hitch knots along the edge-warp thread (see figures 33 and 34). To keep the knots straight, alternate between passing the needle to the left and right sides of the edge-warp thread. To make a picot, just leave a little thread between knots so you have a little loop sticking up to create the picot.

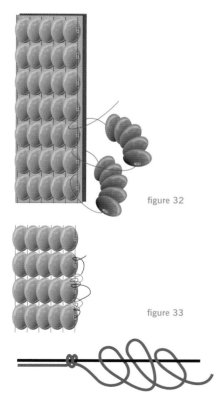

figure 32

figure 33

figure 34

Connecting the Dots

In this surface embellishment, beads are strung across the surface of the loom work by using points on any color pattern as guides. Anchor your thread in the loom work. Then, referring to the pattern points, string on a number of beads, pass through a loom-worked bead, and pull snug (see figure 35). Repeat as desired.

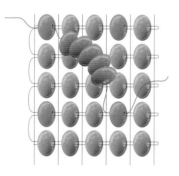

figure 35

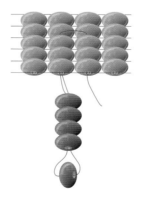

figure 36

Fringe

Adding fringe can transform any project from pleasant looking to downright magnificent and is the best way to include a touch of your own personality and style. Whether a fringe brings just a touch of interest to your loomed piece or is an over-the-top focal point, it should always add a bit of fun. Anything goes when it comes to fringe.

Simple Strand Fringe

The simplest fringe consists of strands of beads that dangle from the ends or edges of your loom work. Use a new thread if you're adding fringe along the edges of the beadwork, or warp threads if you're adding it to the ends. String on the desired number of beads, push the last bead aside (this will be the stop bead) and pass the thread back through all the rest. Then pass through the beads along the edge of the beadwork and exit through the next appropriate bead to make the next fringe (see figure 36).

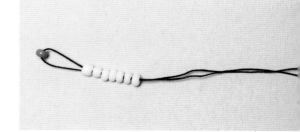

Strand fringe

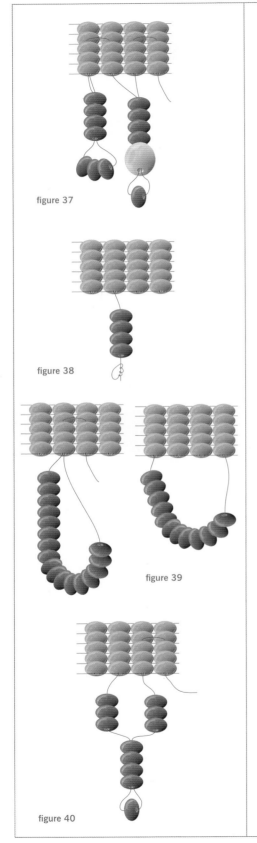

figure 37

figure 38

figure 39

figure 40

Strand Fringe Variations

GRADUATED STRAND FRINGE—To create a more interesting fringed shape, strand fringe can be altered along its bottom edge so that the fringe shape arcs or angles. Just alter the number of beads in each strand.

TIPPED STRAND FRINGE—Work a strand fringe with a larger bead or series of beads at the end of each strand (see figure 37). Fringe can also be tipped or embellished with seed beads applied with needle-weaving stitches.

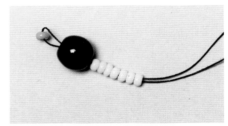

Tipped strand fringe

KNOTTED FRINGE—When using heavy threads that won't pass through the beads, tie a knot at the end of each strand instead of using a stop bead (see figure 38). The Iris Nouveau and Lotus Choker (see pages 51 and 44) illustrate this technique.

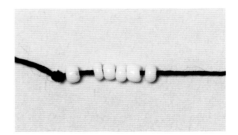

LOOPED (AND SWAG) FRINGE—Create beaded loops by stringing twice the number of beads required for the desired strand length, and weaving the thread end back through the bead you exited from (see figure 39). To create a swag, just pass through a different bead farther along the loomed row.

TWO-LEGGED FRINGE—With your thread coming out of the beadwork, string on the desired number of beads for the first leg of the fringe and for the length of the strand below it. Push the stop bead aside and run back up through the strand beads you just added. Pull all the beads tight. String on the beads for the second leg, and run the thread back into the beadwork not far from the first leg (see figure 40). Repeat along the edge. The Light Shade Skirt on page 80 includes this type of fringe.

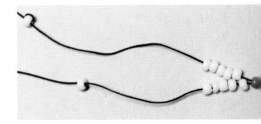

Special Fringe

For a more sophisticated look, try one of the fringe techniques described in this section.

PEYOTE FRINGE—Adding a few peyote stitches (see page 42) along the length of a strand fringe will add pizzazz and a little bit of curl to your fringe.

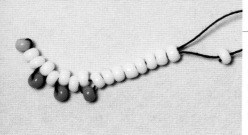

Blue beads are the peyote stitches in this strand fringe.

Start by stringing beads to the desired length of the fringe. Push the stop bead aside, and pass back through a few beads. Then continue up the length of the strand by working a few peyote stitches in the appropriate colors where you want this embellishment. For different effects, alter the bead count and the colors.

To end the effect, pass the thread back through the strand and into the beadwork. Pass through the beads along the bottom edge of the beadwork, and exit through the next appropriate bead for the next fringe (figure 41).

FLOWER-AND-LEAF FRINGE—Create

a strand fringe as usual, incorporating the color pattern provided into the length of it, and exiting at the point where the embellishment will begin.

Then string the appropriate number and color of beads as indicated on the graph, passing through the bead (or beads) indicated. Once the embellishment is complete, pass the thread back through the strand and into the beadwork. Pass through the beads along the edge of the beadwork, and exit through the next appropriate bead for the next fringe (see figure 42).

SPLIT-WARP FRINGE—By using the

split-warp technique (see page 25), you can create fringe with the loom work itself. Divide the warp into sections and work each

one separately. Warp-weave the ends to finish. (Warp weaving stiffens the tension of the loom work; weave all the warps up into the body of the work so the entire fringe is consistent in tension.)

RAW-STRAP FRINGE

With a new thread exiting the beadwork, string on three beads, passing back to exit the second of the three just added. Now work RAW (see the Single-Angle Right-Angle Weave instructions on page 42) for the desired length.

For a single-row fringe, pass the thread back through all the sets of beads and back through the last row of the loom work, exiting where you want to start the next fringe.

For a multiple-row fringe, work a single row down to length. Then work the second row upward onto the first row, borrowing a bead from the edge of the beadwork at the top for an anchored row; or simply make a U-turn and begin a new row for a loose, unanchored row. Work consecutive rows in the same way, ideally ending by burying the thread back into the loom work.

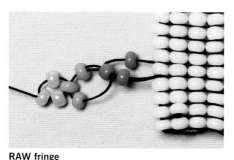

RAW fringe

figure 41

figure 42

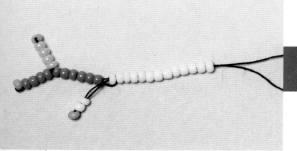

Stiff branch fringe

BRANCH FRINGE—String beads to the desired length of the fringe. Push the last (stop) bead aside, and pass back through a few beads.

String on a branch, push aside the stop bead at its end, and pass back through these branch beads. For a stiff branch fringe (see figure 43, left), pass back through the bead on the main strand that you exited from when you started the branch. (Passing through this bead again will tighten the tension, causing the branch to extend stiffly.) For a loose, grass-like fringe, instead of passing back through the main-branch bead when you've finished the branch, keep the tension loose by passing through the next bead on the main strand (see figure 43, right). Add branches in random positions, working in the same fashion all the way up the fringe.

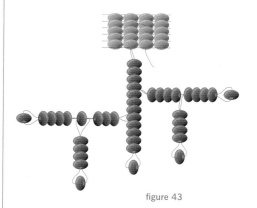

figure 43

To knot or not to knot—that is the question. Believe it or not, you could work a whole piece of loom work without tying a knot; the tension between the beads and the thread would hold everything in place. However, knowing how to tie a knot is useful in many steps other than the loom work itself and will save you time; sometimes tying a simple knot will serve you better than weaving in several inches of thread. Don't stick to a hard-core rule; just do what works best.

Slide Knot

To slide almost any knot into place, insert a needle, pin, or awl into the loop before pulling the knot tight. Close the loop around the tip of the tool, and use the tip to slide the knot into position, usually up to a bead or clasp.

Making a slide knot takes a bit of practice! Kinking your beads or slipping even slightly with your knotting tool will leave a gap between the tip and the beads on the finished piece. Before you let go of the tool, double-check the spacing of your beads.

Overhand Knot

Cross the thread over to form a loop, just as you do when you tie your shoes (see figure 44). Pull tight.

figure 44

Wrapped Knot

Begin an overhand knot, but cross the tail over a few more times before pulling tight to form the knot (see figure 45).

figure 45

Surgeon's Knot

To make a surgeon's knot, first make a wrapped knot; then tie a second overhand knot (see figure 46).

figure 46

Half-Hitch Knot

Half hitches are basically overhand knots tightened around a thread—usually around an edge-warp thread. Pass the thread under the edge-warp thread, cross it over itself, and pull tight (see figure 47).

figure 47

THREAD STITCHES

A few sewing stitches will prove useful to you as you incorporate fabric, hide armatures, and attach one section of beadwork to another.

Running Stitch

With the end of your thread knotted and secured, pass the needle through your fabric up and down in tight even stitches (see figure 48).

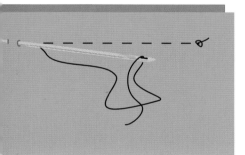

figure 48

Baste Stitch

Work baste stitches as you would running stitches, just make them wide and loose (see figure 49).

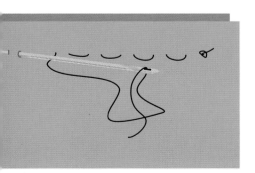

figure 49

Whipstitch

Use a whipstitch to sew the edges of two or more layers of fabric together. Just pass the needle through them at a slight angle, in evenly spaced stitches along the edge (see figure 50).

figure 50

The whipstitch can also be used to attach loom work to layers of fabric. Start by knotting the end of the thread and burying the knot on the inside of the backing material. Exit between rows, bringing the needle up behind the edge-warp thread. Pull tight. Work the stitches between each row of the beadwork.

WHIPSTITCHING BEADED CORNERS— Whipstitch up to the corner, and stitch once before the corner bead. Work a second stitch in the same place, but exit on the opposite side of the corner bead. Work two stitches after the corner bead. This stitch is used in the Signals Coasters on page 85.

BEAD STITCHES

You'll use the stitches described here to attach two pieces of beadwork together and to embellish the surfaces of leather and fabrics. In this section, you'll also find instructions for the classic peyote stitch.

BACK/WHIPSTITCH—Work a whipstitch, adding three beads to it. To begin each stitch, first pass through the last bead of the three added previously, then add three more beads (see figure 51). Once all the beads are added to the edge, pass the needle back through all the beads to straighten them up. (See the Guitar Strap on page 97.)

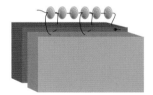

figure 51

Zipper Stitch

The zipper stitch is used to sew the ends or edges of beadwork together. (See the Trillium Rings on page 82.) Start with the thread exiting a bead at the end of a row. Position the opposite end of the loom work next to the working row. Pass the needle back and forth through alternate beads on the two rows (see figure 54). When you reach the end of the row, turn around and pass back through in the same fashion, using the beads that were not used in the first pass. Weave in the tail of thread.

figure 52

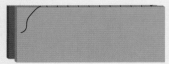

figure 53

Back Stitch

You'll use this stitch to sew beads onto the surface of fabric or leather; the Lolita mirror on page 112 is a good example. Knot your thread and bring the needle up through the fabric where you'd like to begin. String on three beads. Pass the needle down through the fabric so the three beads lay along the surface in a straight line. Bring the needle up through the fabric and pass through the last bead just added (see figure 55). Repeat to create a pattern.

Single-Needle Right-Angle Weave

This stitch, abbreviated as "RAW," is used in the Amulet Bag on page 108. Tie four beads into a circle, then run your needle through one of them (figure 56). *String on three

beads. Now run back through the borrowed bead of the first circle, and then through the next two beads of the three beads just added (see figure 57). Repeat from * to create another circle, then continue to repeat until you have the desired length.

To begin a new row next to the first one, string on three beads. Run back through the borrowed bead along one side of the previous circle and then through the three added beads again. Run through the next bead to be borrowed from the next circle in the previous row (see figure 58).

To continue the new row, *string on two beads. Run through the two borrowed beads, through the two just added, and then through the next bead to be borrowed on the next set of the previous row. Repeat from * to the end of the row. Work as many rows as indicated in the pattern.

tip: To work RAW onto a loomed project, bury the thread in the work and use a bead in the loom work as one of the four beads in the first set.

Peyote Stitch

String on the desired number of beads, as indicated in the project. These will make up the first and second rows of beads. *String on one bead, and using the illustration [below] as a guide, run back through a bead in row 2, in the opposite direction (see figure 59). Repeat from * to the end of the row.

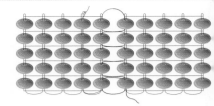

figure 54

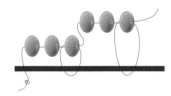

figure 55

figure 56

figure 57

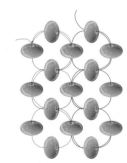

figure 58

figure 59

Jewelry Projects

Forget hard metal and precious stones: these beaded designs
will transform an everyday outfit into a one-of-a-kind look.

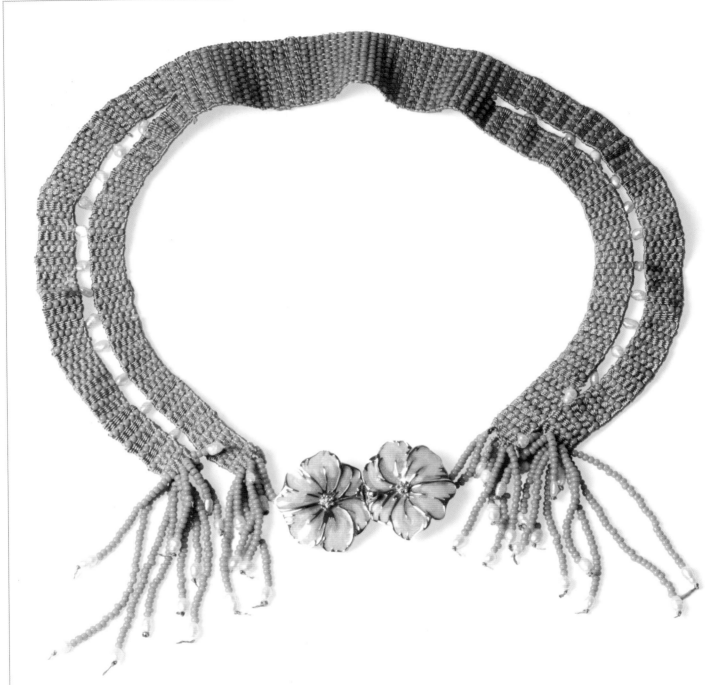

Lotus Choker

Created with luxurious silk thread and freshwater pearls,
this choker begs for a linen blouse and a seaside locale.

beading materials

- Spool of silk
- Strand of pearls
- Tube of 11/0 Japanese seed beads
- Fancy clasp
- Package of wire needles
- Size 9 beading needle
- Size 12 beading needle
- Beading thread

techniques

- Knotted terminal (page 29)
- Wrapped knot (page 40)
- Knotted strand fringe (page 38)
- Adding a clasp (page 32)

instructions

BACK OF THE STRAP

1 Warp a loom with 12 silk warp threads. Using the #9 needle, weave 12 rows of 11 beads. This section will stabilize the necklace at the back of the neck.

2 On each side of the 12 rows, weave 12 rows with four rows of weaving in between them.

SPLIT STRAPS

3 Beginning at the end of step 1, weave two split straps five beads wide. The inner strap will be 32 rows of beads with eight rows of weaving between them. The outer strap will be 37 rows of beads with eight rows of weaving in between them. Repeat on the opposite side of the back strap.

PULLING THE THREADS

4 Cut the work off the loom, leaving as much length as you can to the warp threads.

5 Pull the two innermost edge warp threads on the inside strap, pushing the beadwork up as you pull. This will push the weaving tightly together, causing the strap to arc. Do this to all four straps. Lay the piece flat and begin shaping the straps into an arc, making sure each side reflects the shape of the other. Pull the inner two warps tight, scrunching up the weft threads. Spread or fan out the outermost wefts. The inner straps will lie flat, and the outer strap will ruffle out. The length will vary somewhat after all the scrunching.

ADDING THE PEARLS

6 Work a knotted terminal at the end of each strap. Leave the two innermost warp threads loose. Use the rest of the warp threads to string seed beads and pearls in graduating lengths. Use a wrapped knot at the end of each strand to keep the pearls in place.

STABILIZING THE STRAPS

7 Using the #12 beading needle and the beading thread, weave into the straps. Beginning at the split, weave through the edges of the straps, adding pearls in between the straps. Weave in a roughly zigzag fashion every third row of beads on the inside strap and every fourth row of beads on the outer strap.

CLASP

8 Use the two unused warp threads to add the clasp, stringing seed beads between the clasp and the terminals. String enough to make the length desired; this gives the fancy clasp a "floating" appearance, with the fringe framing it at the base of the neck when worn.

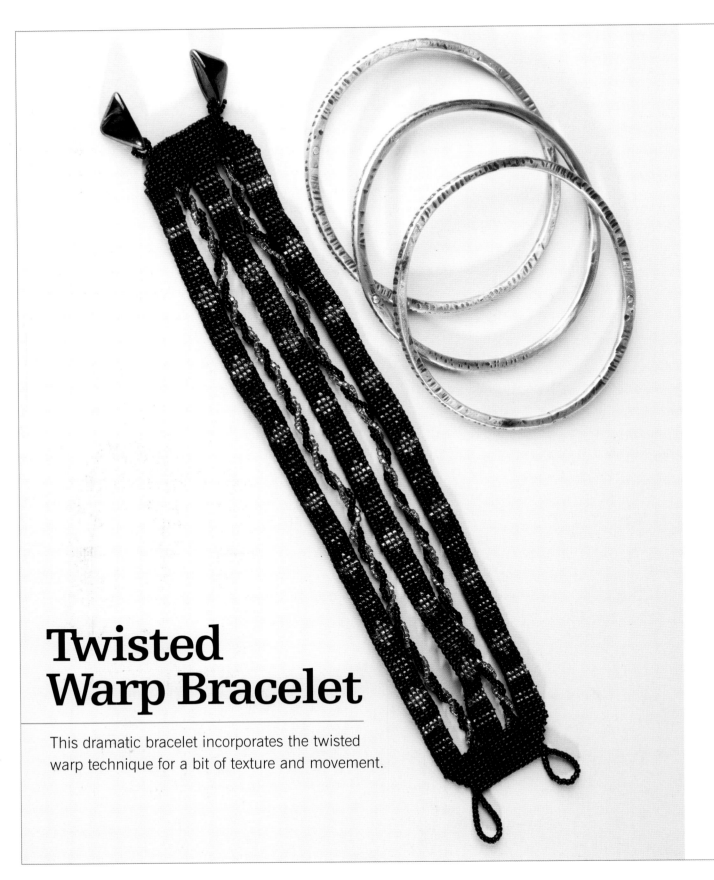

Twisted
Warp Bracelet

This dramatic bracelet incorporates the twisted
warp technique for a bit of texture and movement.

beading materials

- Tube of 15/0 beads for each color in the graph
- 2 clasp beads
- Beading thread
- 3 size 12 beading needles
- Sleigh loom

techniques

- Pointed terminal (page 30)
- Adding a clasp (page 31)

instructions

1 Warp the loom for three straps spaced evenly about ½ inch (1.3 cm) apart across the bridge of the loom.

2 Weave three straps 1 inch (2.5 cm) shorter than the desired length of the bracelet.

3 Add four warp threads to each of the two spaces between the straps.

4 Weave a seven-row terminal at one end, following the graph for decreases.

5 Cut four of the new warps on the opposite end from the weaving. Weave three of each set of new warps into the work, leaving one of the center ones unwoven. Using the single warp thread, string enough of the base color to reach 15 beads past the end of the straps. String an equal amount of the brightest color in the graph. Weave the warp thread into the beadwork, leaving the loop of seed beads hanging out of the way. Repeat on the second set of four new warps.

6 Twist each of the loops by placing a needle into the last black bead at the end of the loop. Turn the needle like a propeller until it's two rows shorter than the straps. Push the needle into the row, pinning the loop in place.

7 String the beads for the first row of the terminal, using the bead at the end of the loop that was pinned in step 6. Weave the rest of the terminal.

8 Remove your work from the loom and warp-weave the threads, using the two outermost ones on each side to weave a clasp.

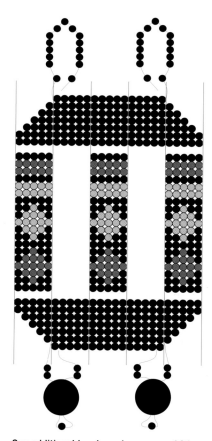

See additional bead graphs on page 124.

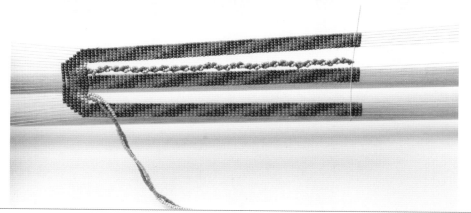

Belle Fleur

Delicate beaded blossoms and subtle
green gradations lend softness and
grace to this stylish lariat.

beading materials

- 2 tubes or hanks of 11/0 seed beads in the base color
- Tube or hank of 11/0 seed beads in gradient color
- Tube or hank each of two different greens
- 1/2 tube or hank for each of the six flower colors
- Needle
- Quilting thread

tools

- Long loom or roller loom
- Scissors

techniques

- Cut warp threads (page 25)
- Flower fringe (page 39)

instructions

note: The lariat will be a long narrow strip of beadwork, with a wider section that forms the clasp of the lariat. Warp the loom for the length of the lariat. You will bead the strap using the tip graph, the repetitive graph, and a transitional graph, if needed.

WARPING

1 Warp your loom for the strap section of the lariat; 12 threads for a strap 11 beads wide. The lariat shown is 56 inches long (142.2 cm) and is worked in sections. The warp threads should be approximately 80 inches (203.2 cm). Begin weaving about 10 inches (25.4 cm) from one end of the threads, leaving plenty of length for weaving the warp ends.

WEAVING

2 Weave the tip section of the strap using the tail to work a pointed terminal. Bead the length of the strap using the repetitive graph (and the transitional graph, if needed).

WEAVING THE CLASP

3 Add seven warp threads on each side of the strap for the clasp of the lariat.

4 Weave the clasp, following the graph for color placement, increases, decreases, and slits. Work the sections in order, weaving the thread through the work to reposition the needle to begin each section.

tip: When working the flower graph, begin the gradient at the seventh repetition. Add a gradient using the second green in the background color.

tip: You can split the strap for added interest. Warp-weave the threads on the end of the strap. Weave a second length for the strap, and use a fringe technique to connect the straps together. To apply a fringe, use one of the beads in the last row of beadwork as a stop bead for the fringe.

Belle Fleur

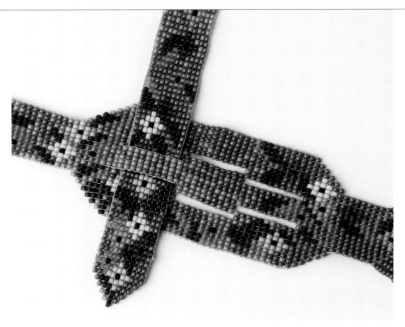

FINISHING TOUCHES

5 Remove your work from the loom, and add fringe along the pointed tip of section 11. Warp-weave any threads that are not used in the fringe and at the tip of the strap.

6 Refer to photo 1 and thread the pointed end of the strap through the slits.

photo 1

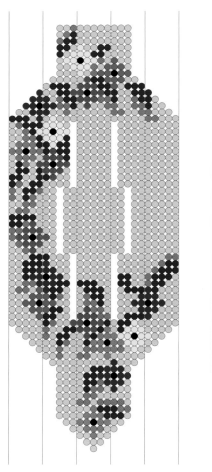

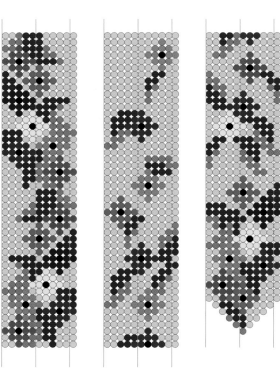

Iris Nouveau

Imagine this fluid piece peeking out from under a collared shirt.

Iris Nouveau

beading materials
- Tube of size 11/0 Japanese beads in the base color
- 1/2 tube of size 11/0 Japanese beads for each of the other colors
- Silk thread or 1 ball of pearl cotton
- Size 9 beading needle
- Crystals or pressed glass beads in multiples of 15 (for the fringe)
- 2 clamshell bead caps
- Clasp finding

other materials
- Liquid seam sealant

tools
- Long loom or a roller loom
- Scissors
- Pin awl

techniques
- Knotted fringe (page 38)
- Split warp (page 25)

instructions

1 Warp your loom for the widest part of the graph. The warps should be 32 to 36 inches long (81.3 to 91.4 cm) from anchor to anchor to give ample thread for warp weaving and fringe in the last steps. When using a roller loom, warp the loom and roll an equal amount of thread on each roller as to begin in the middle. Starting in the middle of the warp, weave the widest part (the body of the necklace). Work the decreases along the bottom to make the shape. Tie off the thread (see page 15 for working silk).

2 Work each strap separately, following the graph. Once the pattern is complete, weave the base color for the length of the strap. Work from the top of the body out along the warps. This is easier to work if you flip your loom around, so you are working as you naturally do rather than working the rows backwards. Repeat for the second strap.

3 Cut the piece off the loom, leaving as much length to the warp threads as possible. Add knotted fringe along the bottom of the body, using two warps per fringe.

4 For a simple edge in the split, weave in the warp threads. For netted edging in the split, use the warp threads to free-form net inside the split.

5 Warp-weave the extra threads at the decreases (if any) along the straps.

6 Warp-weave all but the center two warps. Use the two center warps to add a clamshell bead tip or a beaded clasp.

Fringe chart

Reading the graph from left to right, string the beads on as indicated for each fringe. Use the warp threads along the bottom of the bib necklace, two per fringe as indicated. Tie a knot at the bottom of each fringe, and trim to 1/8 inch (3 mm). Add a drop of liquid seam sealant to each knot.

FRINGES 1 THROUGH 4

Use two of the warp threads, adding the fringe to the corner of the stepped decrease.

FRINGES 5 AND 6

String beads onto the first warp thread. Pass the second warp through all but the first bead of fringe.

FRINGE 7

String beads onto the first warp thread. Pass the second warp through all but the first three beads of fringe.

CENTER FRINGE 8

Use two warp threads with no variation to hang evenly on center bead.

FRINGE 9

String beads onto second warp, and pass the first thread through all but the first three beads.

FRINGES 10 AND 11

String beads onto the second warp, and pass the first thread through all but the first bead.

FRINGES 12 THROUGH 15

Use two of the warp threads, adding the fringe to the corner of the stepped decrease.

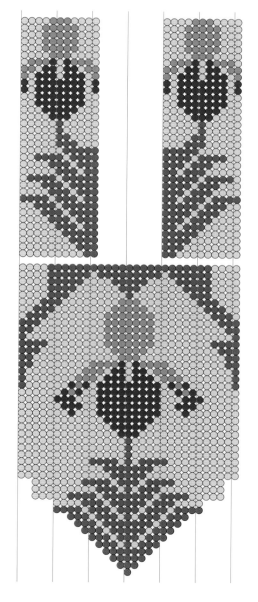

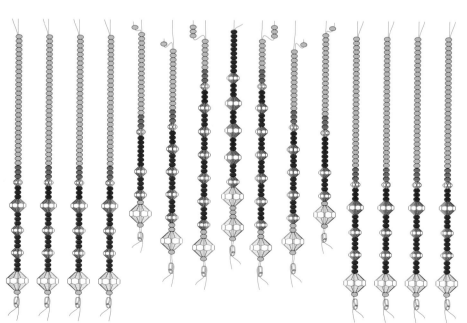

Ganots

A quick knot lends
a pleasing design
element to these
simple earrings.

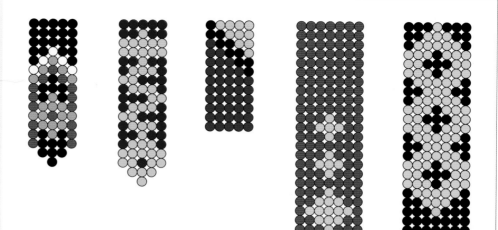

beading materials
- Small amounts of Delica, Magnifica, or 15/0 seed beads
- Needle
- Thread
- Earring wires

tools
- Pin loom
- Scissors

techniques
- Using a pin loom (page 140)
- Attaching metal findings (page 32)

instructions

WEAVING

1 Warp the loom and weave the pattern, following the graph. Work 30 more rows of the base color. Weave in the warp threads and the weft thread at the beginning of the pattern. If the weft thread at the end is too short to work with, weave that in and add a new thread.

MAKING THE LOOP

2 To make the looped bail for the earring wires, begin with the weft thread coming out of the end of the last row. String on five beads (seven beads if using 14/0), and pass the needle through the next row.

To create the loop for the knot, count up to the 15th row from the bottom, and pass through row 15 and then row 16 and then back through the last row of the strip. Pass through the new beads and the two rows again to reinforce the loop (figure 1). Tie off the thread.

3 Repeat steps 1 and 2 for a second earring, but work the loops in the opposite direction.

KNOT

4 Bring the end of the strap up around the front or back and through the loop. Pull through and gently ease the strap through to tighten the knot (photo 1).

5 Add earring findings.

photo 1

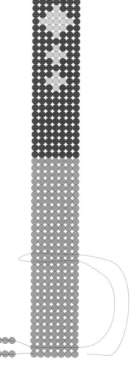

figure 1

Broken Warp Necklace

Multiple strands of beads are the star element in this fabulous piece.

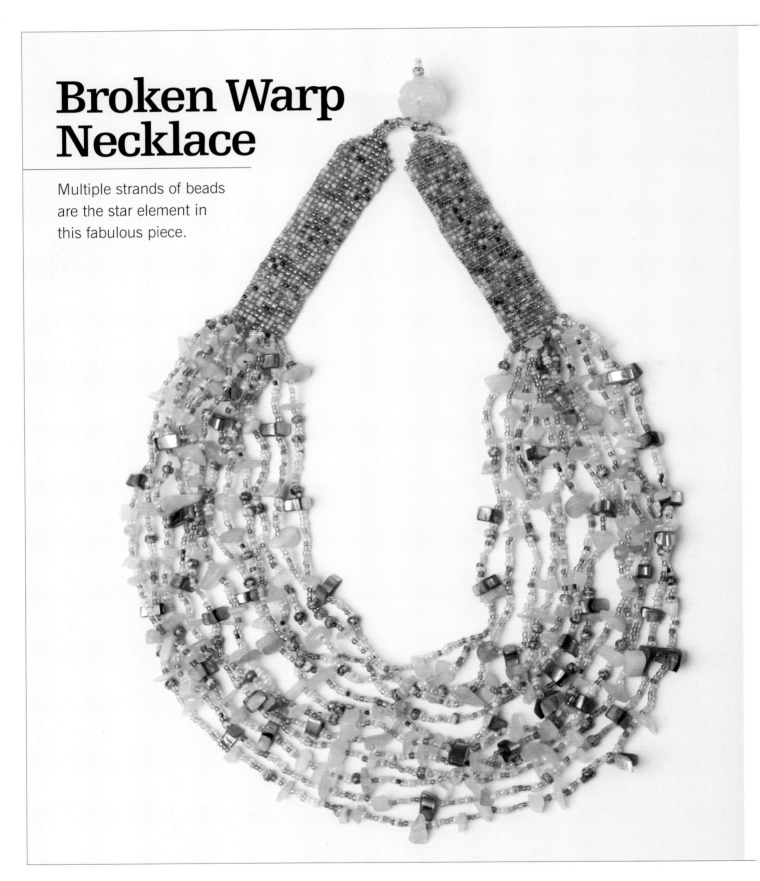

beading materials

- ¹/₂ cup of confetti 11/0 seed bead mix
- Assortment of stone chips, 8/0 beads, and/or pearls

other materials

- Blunted needle
- Thread
- Button or bead for clasp

techniques

- Warp weave (page 28)
- Bead and hook catch (page 31)
- Confetti pattern (page 13)

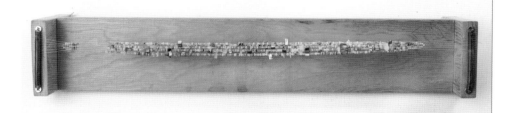

instructions

1 Thread a needle with 3 or 4 yards (2.7 or 3.6 m) of thread, and attach the ends to the anchor of the loom. String the stone and seed bead mixture. To determine the amount of bead mixture to string onto the first warp, first figure out how long you're going to make the beadwork sections at the beginning and end of the necklace. Subtract the lengths of both sections of beadwork from the desired length of the finished pieced, and then string enough beads to equal this length onto the warp thread. Each warp thread should be at least 10 inches (25.4 cm) longer than your desired necklace length. Attach the strung thread onto the anchor on the opposite end.

2 String the beads for the next warp thread, using more beads than you did for the first strand, and attach to the anchor at the opposite end. Repeat until the thread is too short for another pass, and tie the end securely. Begin again with a new thread, repeating until you have 14 warp threads strung.

3 Push the strung beads aside to clear one end of the warp threads for the first section of weaving. Weave one end of the necklace with just the 11/0 seed beads.

4 Push the strung beads into the center so they rest near the first beadwork section. Weave the second beadwork section at the other end of the necklace.

5 Remove the work from the loom, and warp-weave the outer threads of one end, saving the center threads for a clasp. Work the clasp bead or button onto that end.

6 Gently pull the warp threads, while pushing the sections of the necklace together on the warp threads. Work slowly and carefully so the work does not get kinked out of shape and the threads do not become stressed or broken. Once the sections are in place with no threads showing between the strung beads, warp-weave the second terminal using the center two warp threads to form the catch half of the clasp.

Fringed Collar

The asymmetrical design of this collar makes it striking whether placed over a turtleneck or worn against bare skin.

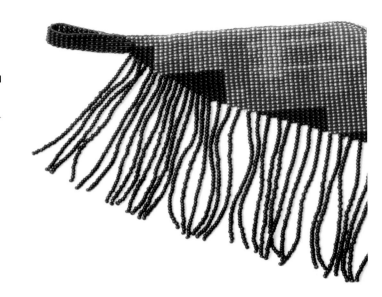

beading materials

- Hank of 11/0 seed beads for each color on the graph
- Needle
- Beading thread

other materials

- Decorative button

techniques

- Pointed terminal (page 30)
- Strand fringe (page 37)
- Strap catch (page 31)
- Decreasing (page 26)

instructions

1 Warp the loom with 50 threads. Beginning in the center of the work space, weave the beads following the graph with the flat side at the bottom of the warp threads. Weave 3 to 4 inches (7.6 to 10.2 cm) of strap, going five beads wide along the flat side and extending the color out. Add a pointed terminal.

2 Once the first half is complete, orient the graph so that the flat side is at the top, and weave the graph again from the wide part out. This may feel somewhat backward, since you will be reading the graph from right to left rather than the normal left to right. Weave 3 or 4 inches (7.6 or 10.2 cm) of strap five beads wide along the flat side, extending the color out. Add a pointed terminal.

3 Use the warp threads along the decreasing sides to add fringe. Make the fringe 35 beads long on the right side and 45 beads long on the left side.

photo 1

photo 2

4 Add a button to one terminal at the end of the five-bead strap (photo 1).

5 Make a catch on the second terminal by folding the strap back on itself and sewing it down to the surface of the beadwork, making sure the loop is large enough for the button to easily pass through (photo 2).

6 Fold the top edge over, and sew the corner down so it's slightly off-center.

7 Work strand fringe along the decreasing edges of the beadwork.

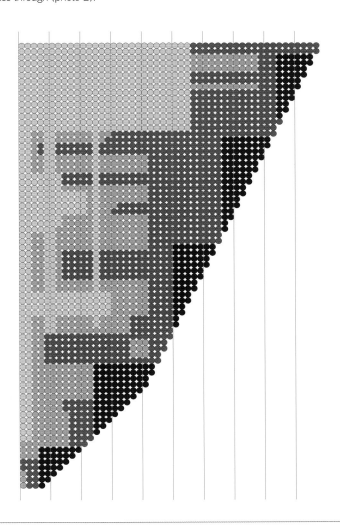

Endless
Straps

As long or short as you desire,
a seamless strap has endless
fashion accessory possibilities.

beading materials

- ½ tube of 11/0 or 15/0 beads for each color on the graph
- Needle
- Thread

tools

- Long or roller loom
- Scissors

techniques

- Connection weave (page 30)

instructions

1 Work a beaded strap, repeating the pattern as many times as will fit in a 36-inch (91.4 cm) length. Go a little shorter or longer as needed to complete the pattern. Remove from the loom.

2 Connect the ends with a connection weave, making sure to not twist the strap.

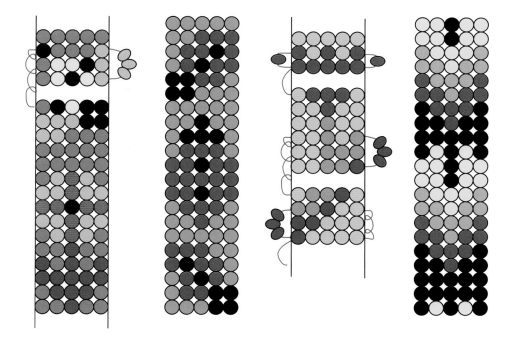

See additional bead graphs on page 138.

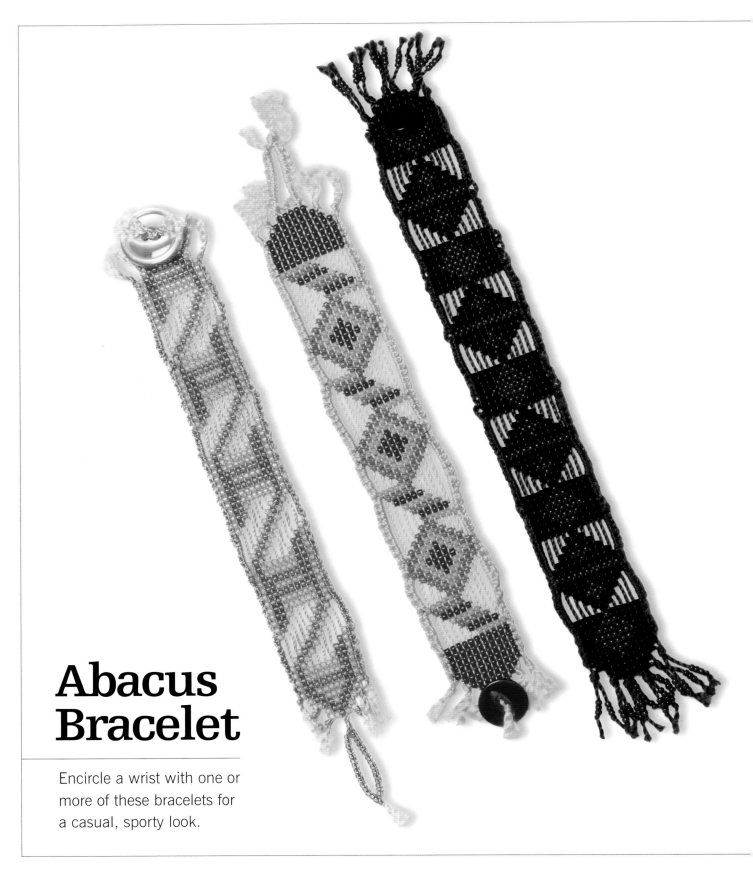

Abacus Bracelet

Encircle a wrist with one or more of these bracelets for a casual, sporty look.

beading materials

- ½ tube of 11/0 seed beads for each color on the graph
- Pearl cotton or other fancy thread
- Darning needle
- Beading needle
- Beading thread in color to match pearl cotton
- Button or large bead for clasp

techniques

- Needle-tatted edging (page 37)
- Slide knot (page 40)
- Working a clasp (page 31)
- Increasing (page 26)
- Decreasing (page 26)

instructions

1 Warp loom with 12 warp threads of pearl cotton.

2 Weave the beads following the graph, leaving open spaces between the beadwork by increasing and decreasing as indicated on the graph.

3 With the beadwork still on the loom, weave a needle-tatted edging along both edges.

4 Remove your work from the loom. Tie a slide knot with every two-warp threads on each terminal.

5 Add beads to each thread of both terminals, and tie a slide knot on each thread. Use the needle or needle awl to split the fibers on the ends, and trim to about ¼ inch (6 mm).

6 With a new beading thread, work a clasp with the hook, bead, or button at one end and the catch at the other.

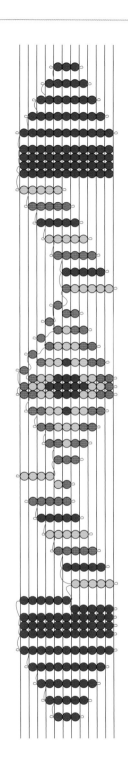

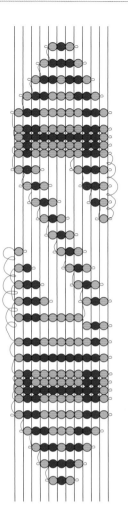

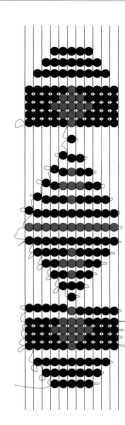

Tag Bracelet

Beadwork goes 3-D with this cool bracelet
that's full of texture and intrigue.

beading materials
- Two 7-gram packs of cylinder beads for each color in the graph
- Size 12 beading needle
- Beading thread

other materials
- Button

tools
- Pin loom
- Sleigh loom

techniques
- Buttonhole catch (page 31)
- Warp weave (page 28)
- Using a pin loom (page 140)

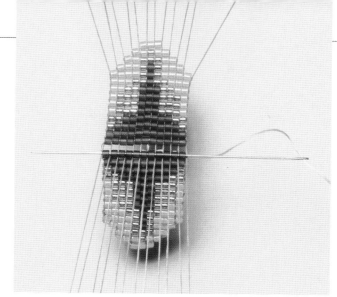

photo 1

instructions

1 Using the pin loom, make tags following the color and shape of the graph (photo 1). The clasp will be approximately 2½ inches (6.4 cm), so to figure the length of the strap, subtract 2½ inches (6.4 cm) from your desired length, and estimate nine tags per inch. Lengthen the clasp to accommodate any variance in the length for the bracelet.

2 Warp a sleigh loom with enough threads to accommodate the number of beads for the width of the graph.

3 Following the chosen graph, weave a terminal at one end of the warp threads, using the same dimensions and colors as for the tags. Alternate one row and one tag to create the length of the bracelet.

4 To weave the tag, slide the needle through the row on the flat end. Push the beads of the row up as you would a row of beads. Take extra care to move the needle over the warp threads on the pass over.

photo 2

5 Create a buttonhole terminal on the second end (photo 2).

6 Warp-weave the terminals at each end, using the two innermost warps of the first end to add the button for the clasp.

See additional bead graphs on page 125.

Cantina Set

No need to go home and change; this dramatic beaded tag set goes effortlessly from day to night.

beading materials

- ½ tube of 15/0 beads or 7-gram package of cylinder beads for each color in the graph (Japanese or Czech beads can also be used but will alter the size slightly. Check the length as you work if you choose to use the other beads)
- 100 round crystals (4 mm)
- Beading wire
- Beading needle
- Machine embroidery thread to match the base color of the beads
- Crimp beads
- Two-strand clasp
- Earring wires

tools

- Pin loom
- Scissors
- Crimp pliers
- Wire cutters

techniques

- Attaching metal findings (page 32)
- Using a pin loom (page 140)

instructions

NECKLACE

1 Weave the tags on the pin loom following the graph. Weave one large tag, two medium, and two small.

2 Use beading wire to string a combination of cylinder beads and crystals, positioning the tags in the center as shown in the photograph.

FIRST STRAND

3 Working with the beading wire coming off the spool, string 22 crystals separated by three cylinder beads.

4 Pass through the top row of the tags, adding one cylinder bead, one crystal, and one cylinder bead between each tag.

5 String 22 crystals separated by three cylinder beads.

6 Add a crimp bead onto the end of the beading wire, pass the wire through the ring bail on the clasp, and then pass the end of the wire back through the crimp bead. Make sure the loop fits loosely around the ring bail. Crimp into place and trim the wire close.

7 Push all the beads toward the crimp bead so there are no gaps. Trim the beading wire 4 inches (10.2 cm) longer than the beaded strand. Attach to the clasp following the instructions in step 6.

SECOND STRAND

8 Repeat the same steps as you did for the first strand except use 24 crystals and pass through the sixth row down on the tags adding two cylinder beads, one crystal, then two cylinder beads between each tag (photo 1).

photo 1

9 String 24 crystals separated by three cylinder beads.

10 Attach to the clasps as you did in steps 6 and 7.

EARRINGS

11 Weave two small tags, adding a loop at the top of each. Attach the loops to earring wires.

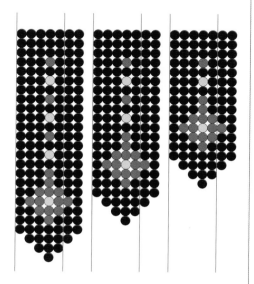

See additional bead graphs on page 125.

Windowpane Bracelet

The unique windowpane effect and a soft edging treatment add textural interest, making this piece a must-have.

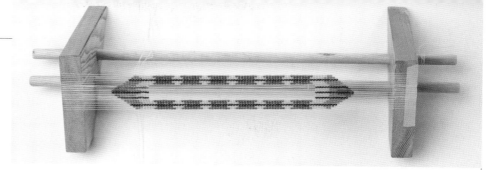

beading materials

- Hank or tube of 11/0 beads in the base color
- Approximately 1 gram of each contrasting color
- Beading thread in a contrasting color that matches the contrasting beads (you want the thread to show)
- Beading needle

other materials

- Toggle clasp
- 2 clamshell bead tips

tools

- Loom
- Scissors

techniques

- Pointed terminal (page 30)
- Warp weave (page 28)

instructions

1 String a loom with 20 warp threads for 19 beads.

2 Weave the sections.

SECTION 1

Work 5 rows.

SECTION 2

Weave a three-bead pointed terminal.

SECTION 3

Cut warp threads seven through 14, and warp-weave them into sections 1 and 2. Weave five bead rows along the left side until you reach the desired length. Note: To figure the length, measure the length of sections 1 and 2. Multiply by two and subtract that from the desired length.

SECTION 4

Weave an equal number of five-bead rows as worked in section 3.

SECTION 5

Add new warp threads to replace the ones that were cut in section 3. Work five rows along the ends of sections 3 and 4.

SECTION 6

Weave a three-bead pointed terminal.

3 Mark every five rows of sections 3 and 4 by running through the row with a contrasting thread, leaving a tail on either side. You'll pull the markers out as you work.

4 With a new thread, work through a few rows of section 1. Exit the first row of section 6 on the inside of the "windowpane."

5 Make the crossbars by stringing beads from one side of the window to the other. Begin at one corner. String 11 beads and pass through every 5th row marked in step 3. Work in one direction to the opposite end, pass through the rows to position the needle into a corner, and work a second pass of crossbars. Pull out all the marker threads.

6 Work a second set of crossbars, working in the same fashion but in the opposite direction.

7 Add a clasp (see page 31).

8 Add an edging if desired (see page 33).

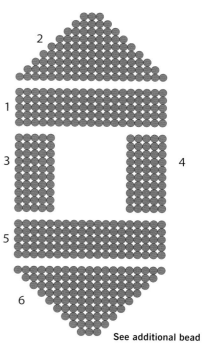

See additional bead graphs on page 126.

Y Necklace

This spirited piece combines daring lines and subtle motion, interspersed with a brilliant gold streak.

beading materials

- Tube each of 15/0 beads in brown, pink, fuchsia, and purple
- Tube or hank of 15/0 gold charlottes
- 4 large gold decorative beads
- Decorative gold fishhook clasp
- 2 gold jump rings (soldered or split)

tools

- Loom

techniques

- Pointed terminal (page 30)
- Warp weave (page 28)
- Adding a metal finding (page 32)
- Branch fringe (page 40)

instructions

1 Weave a strap following the graph. Weave 13 inches (33 cm) in brown, and begin working the gradient colors into the background of the pattern. Weave approximately 1 inch (2.5 cm) of pink, 3 inches (7.6 cm) of fuchsia, and 5 inches (12.7 cm) of purple. Weave a pointed terminal in gold at each end. Warp-weave all but the two innermost warp threads into the work.

2 Add the clasp to the brown end by making two loops with the two innermost warp threads. To make each loop, string on seven beads and pass through a jump ring or the ring bail of the clasp. Bring the thread around the weft thread between the beads of the point of the beadwork. Pass through all again, and then warp-weave the thread (photo 1).

photo 3

3 To add the catch for the clasp, warp-weave a new thread into the strap approximately 5 inches (12.7 cm) up from the purple end. Make sure you're exiting to the inside of the strap. For each loop, string on seven beads, pass through the jump ring, and weave back into the beadwork. Weave through the beadwork to exit next to the first loop. Make a second loop. Exit to the outside of the strap behind the catch (photo 2).

photo 2

4 Add a cluster of branch fringe along three rows. Work shorter branch fringe on the beads of the row, and longer ones exiting from the bottom of the last bead in the row. Add large gold beads to the branches worked on the edge of the beadwork (photo 3).

photo 1

5 Use the two innermost warp threads to add a large gold bead to the end of the pointed terminal.

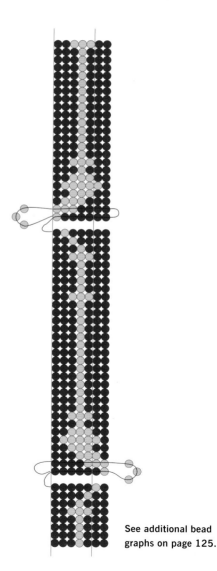

See additional bead graphs on page 125.

Free Spirit Pin

Add a pop of color to your favorite denim jacket or handbag with a sweet little pin.

beading materials

- 11/0, 15/0, or cylinder beads for each color on the graph
- Needle
- Thread

other materials

- Pin finding
- Ultra suede, felt, or leather
- Medium or heavyweight interfacing
- Flexible glue
- Glue stick or two-sided tape

tools

- Loom
- Pencil
- Craft knife

techniques

- Taped, woven, or pointed terminal (page 28)
- Whipstitch (page 41)

instructions

1 Work a strip of beadwork following the graph. Finish with a blunt or pointed terminal. Warp-weave the warp threads for a pointed terminal. Work a woven or taped terminal for a blunt/flat end.

2 To make an armature, glue the interfacing to a piece of leather, ultra suede, or felt. Cut two pieces of armature to the width of the beadwork. If you're working a pointed terminal, trace the ends and cut both pieces to the shape traced.

3 Trim the interfacing 1/8 inch (3 mm) smaller on all sides than the leather or ultra suede. Do this to both armatures.

photo 1

4 Center the pin finding on top of one of the armatures, and trace around to mark the ends. At each end, cut slits through both layers with a craft knife.

5 Push the ends through the slits, coming from the interfacing side.

6 Place a small amount of glue on the interfacing of the armature and between it and the pin finding.

7 Place the two pieces of armature together (photo 1) and weight with a beanbag. Allow to dry.

8 Use the whipstitch to sew the beadwork to the armature, passing only through the two layers of fabric or leather.

9 Add an edging if desired.

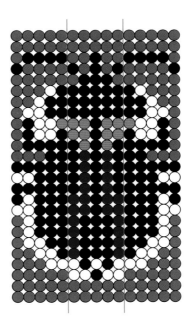

See additional bead graphs on page 126.

Home Decor Projects

Whether it's a bookmark peeking out between the pages of a bestseller, an elegant light pull dangling from your ceiling fan, or chic coasters chilling under your glasses, you can fill your home with unexpected beaded touches.

Bestseller

When it's time to shut off the light, slip a colorful bookmark between the pages to mark your spot beautifully.

Bestseller

beading materials
- Tube or hank of size 11/0 beads for each color in the graph
- Needle
- Thread
- Two 8/0 beads
- Large pendant bead

tools
- Short loom
- Scissors

techniques
- Pointed terminal (page 30)
- Edging (page 33)

figure 1

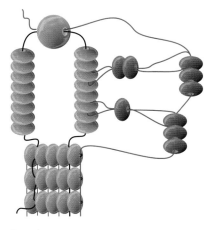

figure 2

instructions

WEAVING

1 Weave a strap of beadwork 6 to 12 inches (15.2 to 30.5 cm) long using the graphs provided.

2 Work a pointed terminal at one end, and warp-weave to finish the bottom of the bookmark.

3 Finish the terminal using the technique appropriate for the pendant bead used.

VERTICAL-HOLED BEAD (Figure 1)

Work a pointed terminal. Warp-weave all but the centermost three warp threads. Use the warp threads to work a chain between the end of the bookmark and the pendant bead.

Thread the two center threads onto needles. String three beads onto one needle and two beads onto the second. Pass the second needle through the third bead. Repeat for length.

Add one 8/0 bead, the pendant bead, and then one 8/0 bead. Pass back through all but the last 8/0 bead, weaving back and forth through the chain and into the beaded strap.

Use the third warp thread to weave a third layer onto the chain, passing through the pendant bead and then back through to the strap.

HORIZONTAL-HOLED BEAD (Figure 2)

Weave in all but the four outermost warp threads, two on either side of the strap. Using the innermost of the two on one side, string on 24 or more beads (in a multiple of three), run through the pendant bead, and string 24 more beads. Weave the warp thread into the beaded strap on the opposite side. Use the inside warp of the opposite side to weave through all the beads that were just added, and reinforce the loop.

Use the edge warp thread to weave a multi-drop edging along the strand, passing through every other bead.

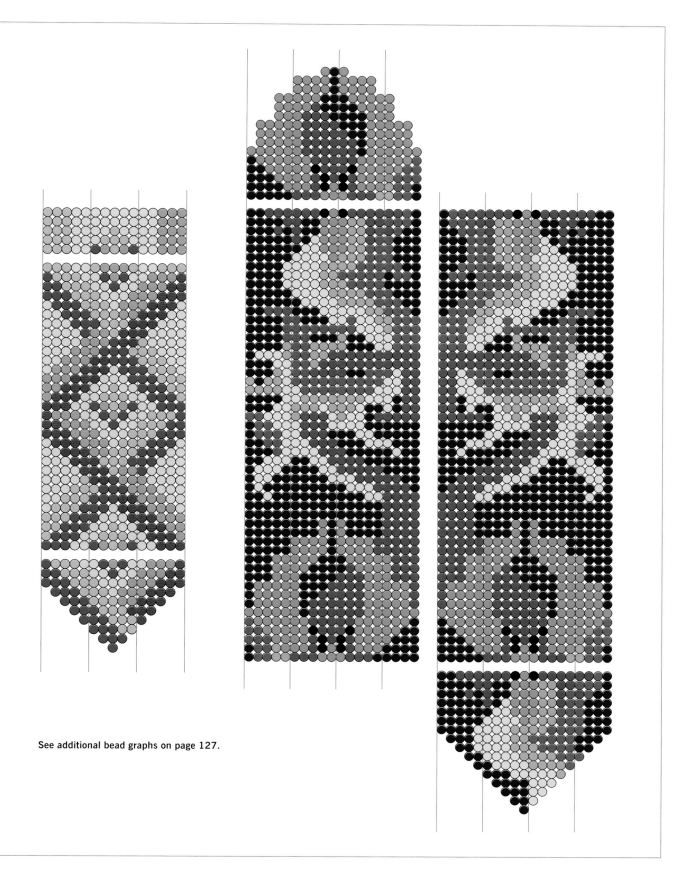

See additional bead graphs on page 127.

Poinsettia Swag

Give plain glass ornaments a makeover with beaded floral coverings.

beading materials

- Tube or hank of red 11/0 seed beads
- 2 tubes of green 11/0 seed beads
- ½ tube of white 15/0 seed beads
- Strand of gold-plated charlottes
- 18 gold-plated 4 mm druks
- Red beading thread
- Needle
- Pin loom

other materials

- Standard-sized glass ornament

techniques

- Using a pin loom (page 140)
- Strand fringe (page 38)
- Swag fringe (page 38)
- Pointed terminals (page 30)

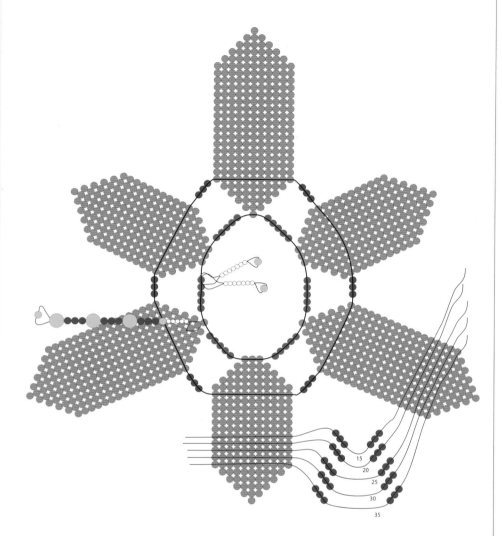

instructions

1 Weave three petals of each size on the pin loom. Small petals are 11 beads wide and 12 rows long. Large petals are 11 beads wide and 17 rows long. Work a pointed terminal on each end of the petals.

2 Weave a new thread into a large petal, and exit though a one-bead point. String five beads between the petals, alternating the three-bead points and the one-bead points. Pass through the first point to form a circle.

3 Weave two strand fringe on each of the beads of the circle. Weave a strand fringe on each point and on the center bead of each three-bead point.

4 Weave thread down to the first 11-bead row on the first petal. String three beads between the petals, passing through the first two 11-bead rows on each petal.

5 String swag fringe between the petals, passing through the last five 11-bead rows on each petal. Use the number of beads indicated on the graph.

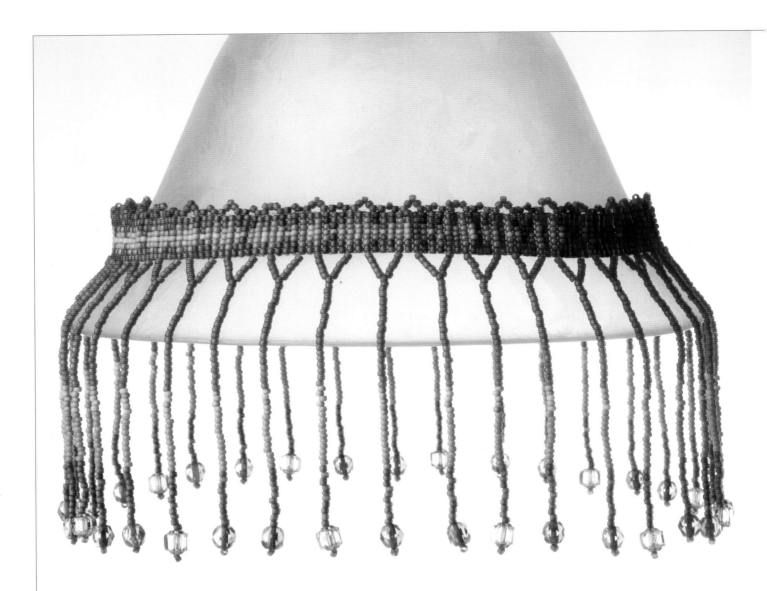

Light Shade Skirt

Dress up a bare light shade with a delicate skirt of beaded fringe.

beading materials

- ¹/₂ tube or hank of 11/0 beads for each color in the graph
- Needle
- Thread
- 36 (or more) faceted 12 mm pressed glass beads

other materials

- Light fixture globe/shade

tools

- Loom
- Scissors

techniques

- Two-legged fringe (page 38)
- Connection weave (page 30)

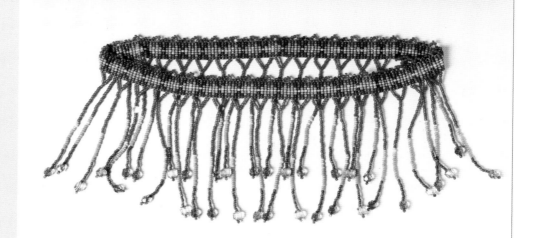

instructions

1 Work a five-, seven-, or nine-bead strap ¹/₂ inch (1.3 cm) shorter than the diameter of the light globe. (The globe in the photo measures 18 inches [45.7 cm].)

2 Work a connection weave to form a circle, making sure to not twist the strap.

FRINGE

3 Work two-legged fringe along the bottom edge of the strap and edging along the top.

String beads in the following order: 25 of color #1, 5 of color #2, 10 of color #3, and 10 of color #4. Add a 12 mm crystal or pressed glass bead and a single seed bead as a stop bead. Push the stop bead aside, and pass up through all of the beads except for the five beads at the top of the fringe. String on five beads of color #1, and pass back through the work.

4 Place the skirt over the top of the globe, letting it rest at an angle. Place the globe into the base of the light fixture.

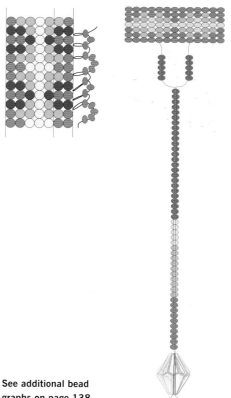

See additional bead graphs on page 138.

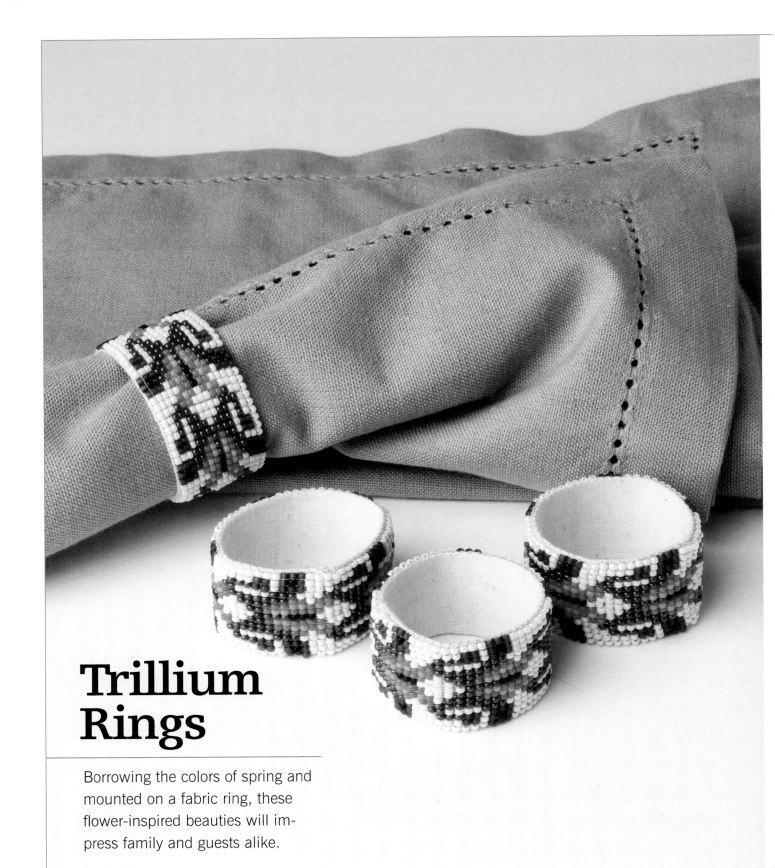

Trillium Rings

Borrowing the colors of spring and mounted on a fabric ring, these flower-inspired beauties will impress family and guests alike.

beading materials

- 1 tube or hank of 11/0 seed beads for each color on the graph
- Needle
- Beading thread

other materials

- Fusible web
- Cardstock
- Cotton fabric
- Sewing needle
- Thread to match the fabric

tools

- Loom
- Scissors
- Iron and ironing board
- Rotary cutter and mat
- Straightedge

techniques

- Taped terminal (page 28)
- Whipstitch (page 41)
- Zipper stitch (page 41)

instructions

1 Weave a strap of beadwork 5 inches (12.7 cm) long and 13 or 15 beads wide. Work a taped terminal at each end.

ARMATURE

2 Cut one piece of fusible web to 8½ X 11 inches (21.6 x 27.9 cm) and another piece to ¾ x 6 inches (1.9 x 15.2 cm). Iron the larger piece onto one side of the cardstock. Cut the fused cardstock to the width of the beaded strap and 6 inches (15.2 cm) long.

photo 1

3 Cut a strip of the cotton fabric to twice the width of the cardstock and 6 inches (15.2 cm) long. Iron the cardstock from step 2, fusible web side down, to the center of the fabric strip, lining up one end. Iron the second strip of web to the cardstock. Fold the long end of fabric over the web and iron it in place, using the fusible web paper to protect your iron from the exposed webbing (photo 1).

4 Once the strip has cooled, clip the fabric corners at each short end to create mitered corners. Fold the sides over, and iron them in place.

ATTACHING THE BEADWORK

5 Lay the beaded strap along the armature with the seam side facing the beadwork. Position the beadwork four rows over the mitered edge. Using a double thread and the sewing needle, sew the edge warp thread to the armature along the long edge using the whipstitch. At the end of the beadwork, tie off. Reattach the thread to the opposite side, and sew the second long edge working in the same direction.

6 Fold the taped terminal under and stitch it to the one side of the strip, keeping the rows of the beadwork even and flat. Fold the second taped terminal under, but do not sew it down. Leave the needle attached.

CLOSING THE RING

7 At the unmitered end with the extra inch (2.5 cm) of covered cardstock, trim the cardstock to make a point that will fit inside the pocket formed by the beaded strap. Thread a beading needle with the beading thread, and attach it to the beaded strap.

8 Bring the ends of the ring together (photo 2). Slide the tab inside the pocket between the fabric and beadwork until the ends of the beadwork come together. Use the zipper stitch to close the ends of the strap together, and tie off.

photo 2

Trillium Rings

photo 3

9 Thread the sewing needle again, and finish sewing the edge down. Run under the beadwork to the other side, and complete that edge. Position the ends so they nestle together without stressing the beadwork, and tack the ends of the fabric in place with a few hidden stitches (photo 3).

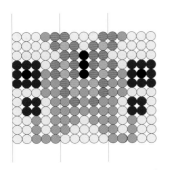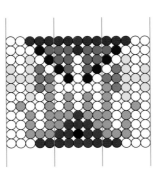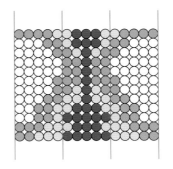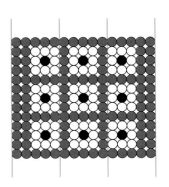

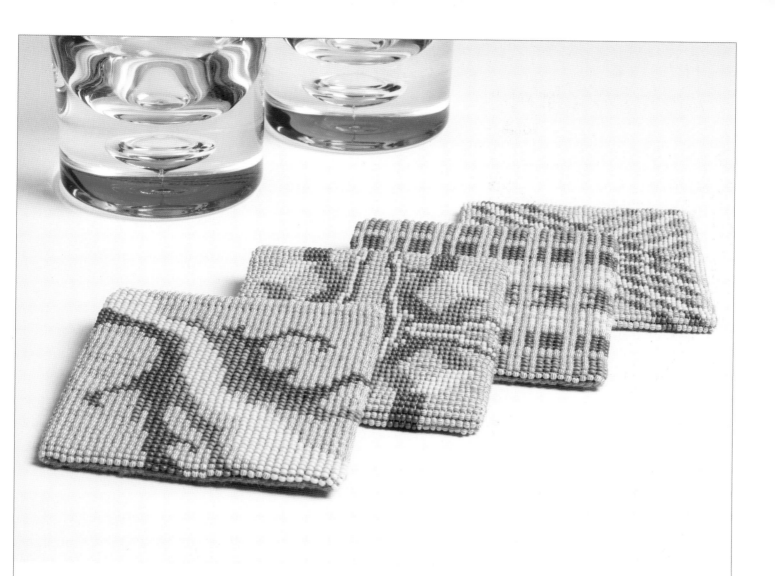

Signal Coasters

You won't have to ask guests twice to use these cool beaded coasters—complete with felt backing and modern geometric designs.

Signal Coaster

beading materials

- 2 hanks or tubes of 11/0 seed beads for each color in the graph
- Ball of size 8 pearl cotton or quilting thread (for warps)
- Beading thread
- Size 12 beading needle

other materials

- 1/4 yard (.2 m) or eight 4 1/2 x 5-inch (11.4 x 12.7 cm) squares of wool felt
- 8 x 10-inch (20.3 x 25.4 cm) sheet or four 4 1/2 x 5-inch (11.4 x 12.7 cm) squares of mat or chipboard
- Fusible web
- Size 9 beading needle or sewing needle
- Spool of sewing or quilting thread to match wool color

Note: Materials listed make a set of four coasters.

tools

- Loom
- Scissors
- Craft knife
- Quilting ruler (see-through acrylic plastic)
- Rotary cutter and mat board (optional)
- Iron and ironing board

techniques

- Woven or taped terminal (page 28)
- Whipstitch (page 41)
- Whipstitch beaded corners (page 41)

instructions

1 For each coaster, warp your loom with 50 warp threads (49 beads). Weave 40 rows following the graphs. Finish the ends with a woven or taped terminal.

2 Cut the felt to match the dimensions of the beadwork.

3 Cut the mat board/chipboard and fusible web into squares 1/4 inch (6 mm) smaller than the felt (1/8 inch [3 mm] on all four sides).

4 Following the manufacturer's instructions, iron a square of fusible web onto each side of the mat board.

5 Position one side of the fused mat board square onto a wool square. Flip the assemblage over and iron the felt, fusing it to the mat board. Test your iron—on the wool setting—on a scrap of wool.

6 Trim the felt to the size of the mat board square. Peel the paper off the second fusible web side.

7 Sandwich the mat board between the two pieces of felt, and iron in place. Cut the points off of each corner.

8 Sew along the edges using whipstitch to attach the beadwork to the squares.

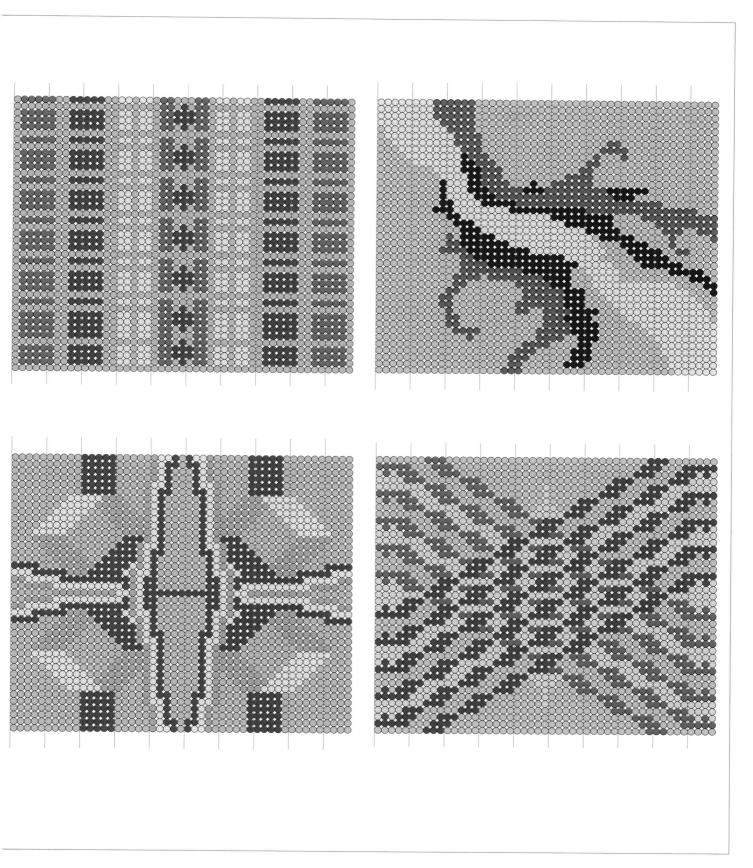

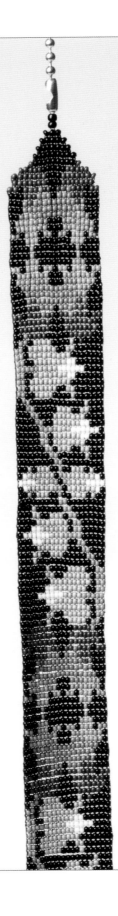

Light Pull

Featuring trailing fuchsias, this fan or light pull is both useful and attractive.

beading materials

- Tube or hank of 11/0 seed beads for each color in the graph
- Size 10 or 12 beading needle
- Beading thread
- Size 9 needle
- Strong UV-resistant fishing line or a braided beading thread that will blend with your colors. (You can use doubled beading thread for this if you can't find a suitable fishing line.)
- Beaded chain clasp
- Three 8/0 beads in the base color

tools

- Loom
- Scissors

techniques

- Pointed terminal (page 30)
- Warp weave (page 28)

instructions

WEAVE THE STRAP

1 Work a beaded strap following the color pattern in the graph.

2 Work a pointed terminal at each end. Warp-weave all the warp threads into the strap.

MAKING THE CLASP

Note: Weaving in a heavier line to hold the clasp will reduce the fraying and lengthen the life of the light pull without making the strap stiff and heavy. By weaving it in without knotting, the line is more likely to pull out without harming the beaded strap, should someone pull too hard on the strap.

3 Thread the size 9 needle with ¹/₂ yard (.5 m) of the fishing line, braided beading thread, or doubled thread. Starting about one-third down from one end of the strap, warp-weave up one side of the center bead, leaving a thread tail a few inches (cm) long. Exit alongside the center bead of the last row. String the three 8/0 beads. Push the last one aside and pass through the other two. Warp-weave down the strap six or eight rows, on the opposite side of the center bead. Pull the thread to bring the 8/0 beads together at the top of the strap. Leave the thread loose. Push the beaded chain clasp over the top 8/0 bead, sliding the thread down through the slit with the bead resting in the "cup" of the clasp.

4 Pull the thread tight so the tension holds the clasp in place. Warp-weave down the strap alongside the center bead, exiting even with the tail where the weave began. Trim the tails close to the bead-work. The tension of the beads and thread together will hold the line in place.

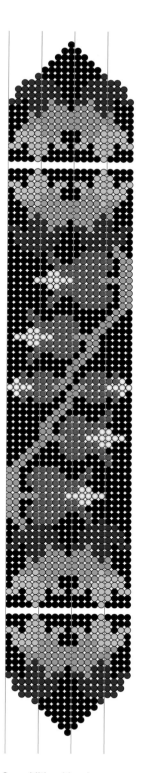

See additional bead graphs on page 128.

Aztec Sky

Why settle for boring plastic switch plates when you can bead one to match every room décor?

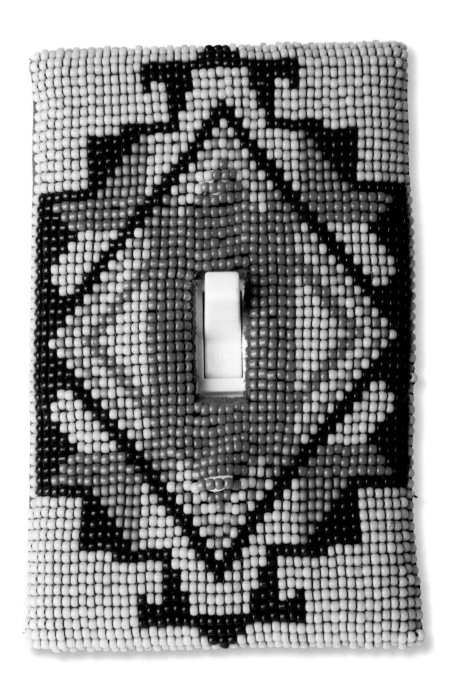

beading materials

- Tube or hank of 11/0 beads for each color on the graph
- Size 10 beading needle
- Quilting thread to match the color of the leather

other materials

- Piece of leather 3 or 4 inches (7.6 or 10.2 cm) larger than the switch plate
- Standard light switch plate
- Nail polish remover
- Contact cement and cotton swabs
- Medium grit sandpaper
- Precut insulating sheet

tools

- Scissors
- Sleigh loom
- Rotary cutter and mat
- Beanbag weights
- Standard screwdriver

techniques

- Taped or woven terminal (page 28)
- Whipstitch (page 41)
- Bridged weft (page 26)

instructions
WEAVING

1 Warp the loom with 48 threads to accommodate 47 beads. Weave the beadwork in sections, following the graph.

SECTION 1

Weave 11 complete rows.

SECTION 2

Warp-weave the six innermost warps, to form a window in the beadwork. Weave 12 rows spanning the window with beads using the bridged weft technique.

SECTIONS 3 AND 4

Weave 13 rows on each side.

SECTION 5

Add in six new warp threads to replace the ones woven in in section 2. Weave 12 rows spanning the window with beads.

SECTION 6

Weave 11 full rows. Remove the beadwork from the loom, and work a taped or woven terminal at each end.

COVER THE SWITCH PLATE

2 Cut the leather to size allowing an extra inch (2.5 cm) or so on all four sides.

3 Sand the surface of the switch plate on the front and back edges, and then clean it with alcohol or fingernail polish remover. Glue the face of the switch plate to the wrong side of the leather. Weight with beanbags, and allow to dry.

4 Trim the leather to 1 inch (2.5 cm) on all four sides. Miter the corners, leaving 1/8 inch (3 mm) of leather at the point of each corner. Fold the leather edges over the switch plate, and glue. Weight with beanbags, and let dry thoroughly.

5 Thread the size 10 needle with a short thread knotted at one end. Sewing through the top layers of leather, sew the corners closed using small, tight stitches. Once the corner is sewn closed, pass the needle under the leather through the point and back under the leather. Pull the stubby tail of the corner in nice and tight (photo 1). Tie a good tight knot. Repeat on the other three corners.

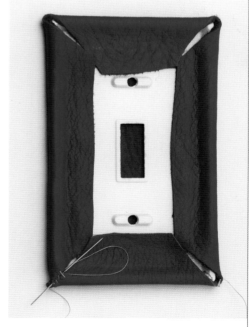

photo 1

Aztec Sky

6 Use a craft knife to trim the leather around the edges, the center, and the screw holes. Scrape off any excess glue (photo 2). Glue down the precut insulating sheet to cover the leather edges.

ATTACHING THE BEADWORK

7 Position the beadwork on the leather, making sure it's centered. Use a whipstitch to sew the leather around the center hole (photo 3).

8 Push the screws into their holes, and position the beadwork over them. Fold the terminals under, and sew the edges of the beadwork to the leather on all four sides.

INSTALLATION

9 To install the light switch cover, remove the old plate and position the beaded cover over the screw holes in the switch. Gently expose the screw head by pushing the bridged weft beads aside (photo 4). Place screw into the hole. Do not force the screw in too far. Repeat on the second screw.

photo 2

photo 3

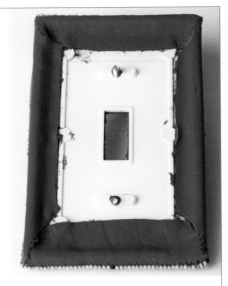
photo 4

See additional bead graphs on page 130.

Accessories

Brighten up your daily routine with these stylish and practical accessories. There's even a snazzy leash and collar so your dog will look as sharp as you do on that early morning walk.

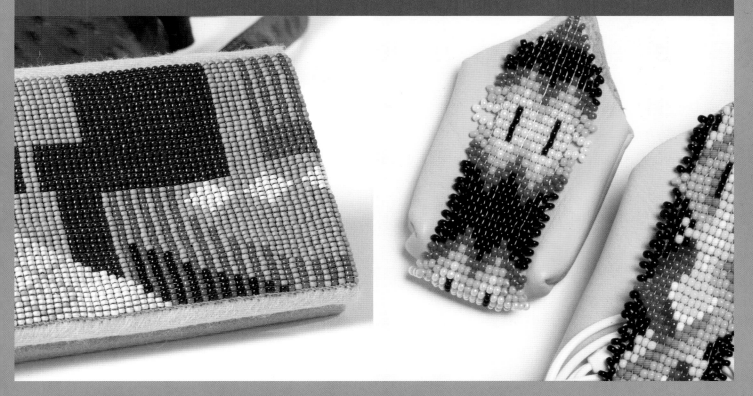

Stellular

Style will be your companion when
you clip this flashy cell phone
holder onto a belt or purse.

beading materials

- ¹/₃ tube or hank of 11/0 beads for each color in the graph
- Beading thread
- Needle

other materials

- Sewing needle
- Sewing thread
- ¹/₄ yard (.2 m) of cotton fabric
- Heavy-duty interfacing
- Holster clasp or fork holster
- Contact cement or glue

tools

- Sleigh loom
- Scissors
- Rotary cutter and mat
- Ruler
- Iron
- Sewing machine (optional)
- Optional tools for fork clasp: hammer and large clamp with a work surface, double-sided tape or straight pins.

techniques

- Woven or taped terminals (page 28)
- Warp intersection (page 24)
- Whipstitch (page 41)

instructions

1 Weave the center bar beadwork following the graph and working woven or taped terminals.

2 Weave the cross bars (5 beads by 15 rows) with the warp intersection technique. Work the first cross bar five rows down from the top, and work the second 20 rows down from the first (photo 1). Work a woven or taped terminal at each end of the cross bars.

CENTER BAR

3 Cut a 3 x 7-inch (7.6 x 17.8 cm) strip of fabric. Fold the top and side edges in so the fabric is the same size as the center bar. Lay the beadwork on top of the bar armature so the tops are lined up. Note: The raw end of fabric will be longer than the beadwork, but do not trim this. This will be the tab that forms the bottom of the case.

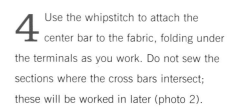

photo 2

4 Use the whipstitch to attach the center bar to the fabric, folding under the terminals as you work. Do not sew the sections where the cross bars intersect; these will be worked in later (photo 2).

BODY

5 Cut a rectangle of fabric that is 1 inch (2.5 cm) wider than twice the span of the cross bars from top to bottom. Fold the rectangle in half with right sides together, and stitch along the raw edge, using a ¹/₂-inch (1.3 cm) seam allowance, to create a fabric tube. Turn the tube right side out and iron it flat.

photo 1

Stellular

photo 3

6 Position the fabric seam side down under the cross bars (photo 2), lining up the top and bottom edges. Hold, pin, or use double-sided tape to secure work in place. Note: The raw end of fabric will be longer than the beadwork at both ends.

7 Sew along the edges using the running stitch, folding under the terminals as you work. Use the hidden stitch to attach the fabric tube where it crosses the fabric-backed center bar.

THE BACK

8 Cut two 2¼ X 4-inch (5.7 x 10.2 cm) rectangles from the interfacing. Sew the holster clasp in place on one sheet of interfacing, adding a little glue between the interfacing and the clasp. Add glue to the center of both pieces and press them together, aligning the edges.

9 Cut two rectangles of the fabric that measure 3½ x 4½ inches (8.9 x 11.4 cm). Sew the pieces together, with right sides facing, along the long edges to create a fabric tube, using a ½-inch (1.3 cm) seam allowance. Turn the tube right side out and iron the seams flat, leaving the bottom and top open.

10 Fold in the edges at one end of the tube. Slide the interfacing and clasp inside the tube, keeping the edges folded under, and sew closed using the hidden stitch. Be sure the clasp is centered and flush with the top (photo 3). Fold the bottom edges in with one side covering over the bottom edge of the interface. Leave open for a later step.

ATTACHING THE BODY TO THE BACK

11 Center the body to the back and sew along the seam. Use a running stitch to sew the bottom edge of the right side of the body to the front right side of the back. Use the hidden stitch to sew the right top edge of the body to the back edge of the back.

12 Sew the left side of the body to the left side of the back in the same fashion.

13 Slip the fabric tab at the bottom of the bar into the folds along the bottom of the back. Stitch in place. Use the hidden stitch to sew the bottom closed.

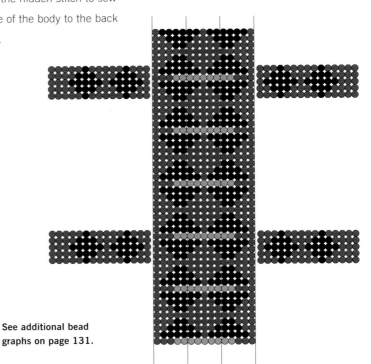

See additional bead graphs on page 131.

Guitar Strap

With custom leather terminals
and holes for the guitar pegs,
this strap is ready for action.

Guitar Strap

beading materials
- 2 tubes of 11/0 beads in each of the dominant colors
- Tube of 11/0 beads for each of the other pattern colors
- Needle
- Thread
- Tape
- Long loom or roller loom

other materials
- Felt or cotton quilt batting
- Webbing at least 18 inches (45.7 cm) longer than the beadwork
- Craft quality buckskin or leather
- Quilt thread
- Sharp needle
- Paper and pencil
- Craft knife
- Glue
- Hole punch
- Rotary cutter and mat (optional)

techniques
- Warp weave (page 28)
- Baste stitch (page 41)
- Whipstitch (page 41)

instructions

1 Warp loom with 30 warp threads. Weave the repetitive pattern for approximately 32 inches (81.3 cm). Weave the terminals at each end. Warp-weave the warp threads.

2 Cut a strip of felt 1/8 inch (3 mm) narrower than the beaded strap, for padding. Baste stitch the felt to the back of the beaded strap, keeping the stitches loose so as to not distort the tension of the warp or weft threads.

3 Using a whipstitch, sew the edges of the beadwork to the edges of the webbing and around the terminal shapes. Leave ample webbing at each end for the leather terminals. Leave 6 inches (15.2 cm) at one end and 12 inches (30.5 cm) at the other for a 36-inch-long (91.4 cm) strap.

4 To prepare the inset for one end, cut the paper to the width of the strap. Lay one end of the paper over the beadwork terminals. Gently rub with the pencil point, embossing the shape of the beadwork terminal onto the paper (photo 1). Cut the paper along the lines to make patterns for cutting the leather.

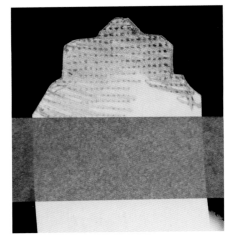

photo 1

5 Cut two equal length strips of leather wider than the webbing and longer than the length needed. Cut one with a straight end. On the second strip, tape the pattern at the end and cut out the terminal shape with a craft knife.

6 Brush glue onto the backsides of each leather strip and sandwich the webbing between them, paying special attention to the insert to make sure the edge of the leather is neatly snuggled up against the edge of the beadwork. The backside leather strip should be even with the edges of the top leather strip. Both strips should be wider than the webbing, so before the glue dries, make sure there will be enough overhang to trim evenly. Weight with a beanbag, and let the glue dry according to the manufacturer's instructions. Note: Many types of glue will not adhere to the polyester fibers of the webbing. I prefer flexible fabric glue.

7 Repeat steps 4 through 6 for the second end.

8 Trim the sides of the leather strips to approximately 1/8 inch (3 mm) wider than the webbing. You should be able to see the webbing embossed into the leather; use that as a guide.

9 Cut a strip of paper to the width of the webbing. Fold it in half lengthwise and cut the end in an arc. Unfold and use it as a pattern to cut the ends of the strap. At one end of the strap, use the arc pattern to cut the end 5 or 6 inches (12.7 or 15.2 cm) from the beadwork. Cut 11 or 12 inches (27.9 or 30.5 cm) from the other end. The strap will be adjustable, so it doesn't have to be exact.

10 Use quilting thread and a sharp needle to sew beads along the leather edge using a back/whipstitch (photo 2).

photo 2

11 Make marks for the holes, spacing them evenly along the leather, and then punch holes with the hole punch. Use a craft knife to cut 1/2-inch (1.3 cm) slits along one point of each hole. These holes will act like buttonholes, allowing the strap to be attached to the strap buttons on each end of the guitar body. Make sure to cut the slits toward the beadwork at each end.

See additional bead graphs on page 132.

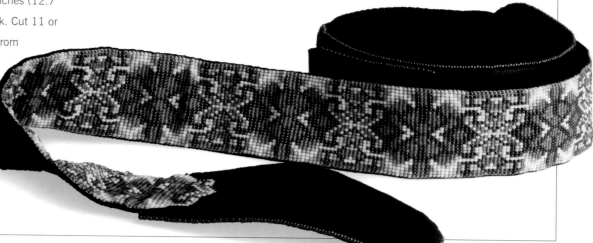

Trailblazer

Create a strand of beadwork and attach it to a store-bought collar for a fun, pet-boutique look.

beading materials

- Tube each of 11/0 seed beads for each color in the graph
- Beading thread
- Needle

other materials

- Polyester webbing
- Thread to match color of webbing
- Sewing needle
- "D" ring
- 1-inch-wide (2.5 cm) buckle
- Swivel snap
- Bias tape or strip of felt (optional)

techniques

- Taped terminal (page 28)
- Pointed terminal (page 30)

photo 1

tip: Position the buckle at the end of the beadwork with the "D" ring 1½ inches (3.8 cm) away from the buckle. Fold the end of the webbing under, and sew into place. The "D" ring will be where the leash is attached (photo 1).

instructions

COLLAR

1 For the collar, measure for your desired length and subtract ¾ of the length of the buckle. Weave a strap the length of the collar. Work a taped terminal at each end.

2 Sew the strap to the webbing, leaving 1½ inches (3.8 cm) of exposed webbing on one end and 3 inches (7.6 cm) on the other (the "D" ring end).

3 Attach the first half of the buckle (see page 33), then attach the other end to the second half of the buckle and the "D" ring.

LEASH

1 Weave one strap the length of the leash. Work a taped terminal on one end (where the swivel snap will go) and a pointed terminal on the other (to make the handle portion).

2 Sew the strap to the webbing. Leave 14 inches (35.6 cm) of the webbing exposed from the point of the beadwork for the handle, and 2½ inches (6.4 cm) from the blunt end to accommodate the swivel snap.

3 Attach a swivel snap. To make the handle, fold the other end under 1 inch (2.5 cm) and sew it down, forming a loop, on the back side of the webbing.

See additional bead graphs on page 132.

Pathways
Checkbook

This dapper checkbook cover will
make bill paying more pleasurable.

beading materials

- 1½ tubes of 11/0 seed beads for each color in the graph
- Needle
- Thread to match base color in graph

other materials

- ¼ yard (.2 m) of wool felt
- Spool of sewing thread to match felt
- ¼ yard (.2 m) of fusible webbing
- ¼ yard (.2 m) of medium-weight interfacing

tools

- Scissors
- Rotary cutter and cutting mat
- Iron and ironing board

techniques

- Taped terminal (page 28)
- Whipstitch beaded corners (page 41)

instructions

1 Weave beadwork following the graph. Work a taped terminal at each end.

2 Measure and cut the following:
Two pieces of wool felt 7 x 14 inches (17.8 x 35.6 cm)
One piece of medium-weight interfacing 6½ x 13 inches (16.5 x 33 cm)
One piece of fusible web 6 x 11 inches (15.2 x 27.9 cm)
One piece of fusible web 6 x 10 inches (15.2 x 25.4 cm)

3 Center and then fuse the 6 x 11-inch (15.2 x 27.9 cm) piece of fusible web to the piece of interfacing following the manufacturer's instructions, being careful not to scorch the felt. Fuse the interfacing to one piece of the wool fabric.

4 Stack the pieces of wool together, lining up the edges to match. Sew the long edge on either side of the fused interfacing with a ¼-inch (6 mm) seam. Iron the second fusible web onto the interfacing, making sure it is centered.

5 Turn the piece right side out, and iron to fuse the second piece of wool to the interfacing.

6 Trim each corner at an angle. Open up the end flaps and trim the seams. This eliminates the extra bulk at the corners. Use the hidden stitch to sew the ends closed, then fold each end over 2¾ inches (7 cm) and sew along the sides.

7 Fold the checkbook in half, and center your beadwork on the front cover. Sew it in place using a running stitch along the warp thread, the edge, and between the beads of the end rows. Add an edging if you want to camouflage the stitches.

tip: Since wool has insulating properties, use the wool setting on your iron rather than the fusible web manufacturer's settings. Check every few seconds to make sure the fusible web is getting hot enough to fuse the pieces together, but is not burning the wool.

Rio Card
Holder

You'll leave a first-
class impression
when you slide your
business card out of
this fashionable case.

beading materials

- ½ tube or hank of 11/0 beads for each color represented in graph

other materials

- Cloth tape
- Wool felt
- Cardstock
- Fusible web
- Needle and thread

tools

- Scissors
- Loom
- Iron
- Ruler
- Craft knife or rotary cutter and cutting mat

techniques

- Woven or taped terminal (page 28)
- Picot edging (page 33)
- Whipstitch beaded corners (page 41)

instructions

1 Weave a strap of beadwork 35 beads wide by 45 rows long. Finish the work with a woven or taped terminal at each end.

2 Cut three pieces of felt to match the dimensions of the woven beadwork.

3 Cut a rectangle of cardstock ⅛ inch (3 mm) smaller than the felt.

4 Iron fusible web, one side at a time, to both sides of the cardstock following the manufacturer's instructions. Do not remove the protective paper.

5 Remove the protective paper from one side of the rectangle of cardstock. Center and fuse the cardstock to one piece of felt. Fuse the second felt rectangle to the cardstock, matching the edges.

6 Trim ⅛ inch (3 mm) from the top of the remaining piece of felt. Trim the felt at an angle from the upper left corner to a little over half the way up from the bottom to form the pocket.

7 Sandwich the felt and woven beadwork together. Stitch three sides together using a running stitch.

8 Add a beaded edge, if desired.

See additional bead graphs on page 134.

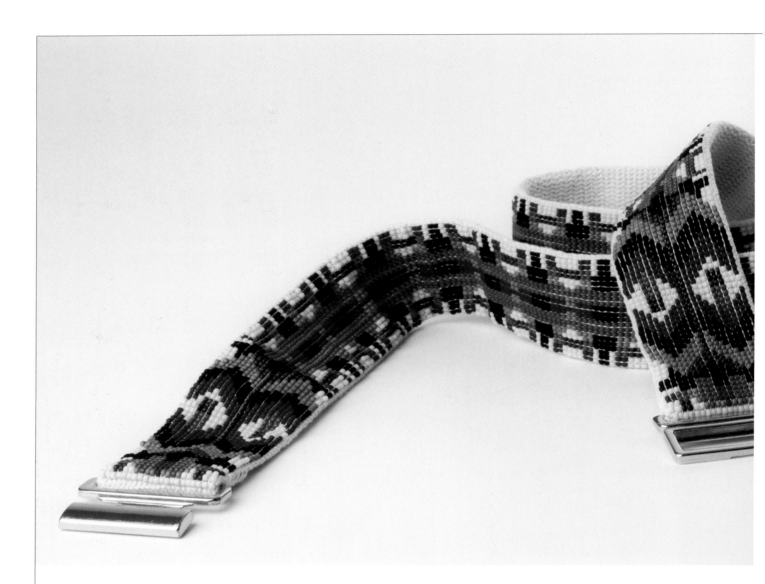

Durango Belt

Weave the perfect accessory for your favorite pair of denims.

beading materials
- Tube or hank of 11/0 beads for each color in graph
- Spool of quilting thread
- Size 10 or 12 beading needle

other materials
- 1½-inch (3.8 cm) metal buckle
- Webbing, 1½ inches (3.8 cm) wide and at least 5 inches (12.7 cm) longer than the desired belt length
- Ball of pearl cotton
- Liquid seam sealant

tools
- Tape measure
- Loom longer than the length of your belt (42-inch [106.7 cm] loom)
- Scissors
- Sewing needle

techniques
- Woven or taped terminal (page 28)

instructions

1 Use the pearl cotton for warp threads. Double up the edge warps.

2 Measure the recipient's waist— your beading will need to be that measurement. The buckle will add enough length so the belt will fit comfortably. Starting in the center and working out to one end, weave the beads according to your chosen pattern. Return to the center and work in the opposite direction. You can add rows of the base color at each end if you need more length.

3 Work a woven or taped terminal.

4 Sew the beadwork to the webbing using a running or whipstitch.

5 Cut the ends of the webbing 1½ inches (3.8 cm) longer than the beadwork. For cotton and natural fibers, secure the fraying ends of the strap with liquid seam sealant. Melt polyester ones with a lighter.

6 Run the end of the webbing over the bail of the buckle. Fold the cut end under so it rests next to the bail. Stitch along the three sides to secure in place.

See additional bead graphs on page 137.

Amulet Bag

This pouch makes an attractive necklace and provides a handy place to
store a photo, ticket, or some cash.

beading materials

- Tube of 11/0 seed beads for background color on the graph
- ½ tube of 11/0 seed beads for each pattern color on the graph
- Needle
- Thread

techniques

- Warp weave (page 28)
- Right-angle weave fringe (page 39)

instructions

1 Warp the loom, and weave following the graph. Warp-weave the ends.

2 Weave a picot edging along both sides of the strip, keeping the tension on the edging loose.

3 Fold the strip in half, and weave the side seams with right-angle weave, borrowing the point beads of the picot from each half of the folded strip (figure 1).

4 Work the fringe as desired, along the bottom of the bag (figure 2). Sample bag: Work graduating strand fringe along the front row. Along the back row and evenly spaced, work 4 single-row RAW fringe on each side with a 4-row RAW Tab Fringe in the center.

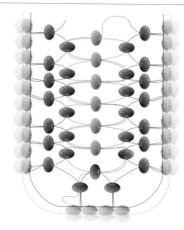

figure 1

figure 2

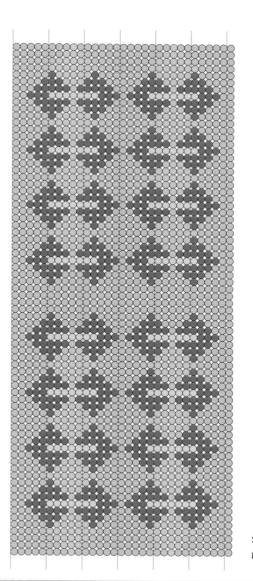

See additional bead graphs on page 135.

Canyon Lands

Hang your keys, security card, or reading glasses from this smart lanyard, and never lose them again.

beading materials

- Tube or hank of 11/0 beads for each color in the graph
- Ball of size 8 pearl cotton
- Beading thread
- Size 10 or 12 beading needle
- Size 9 beading needle

other materials

- 4-inch (10.2 cm) square of leather
- Glue (contact cement or flexible fabric glue)
- Grommet
- Small key ring
- Lanyard clasp

tools

- Roller loom (or 60-inch [152.4 cm] long loom)
- Scissors
- Circle template
- Pen
- Mat
- Grommet-setting tools (hole punch, setting die, rawhide or rubber hammer)
- Split-ring pliers

techniques

- Netted terminal (page 29)
- Connection weave (page 30)
- Tombstone terminal (page 27)

instructions

WEAVING

1 Warp the loom, and weave 12 repetitions of the 3-inch (7.6 cm) pattern graph. Remove the weaving from the loom, and work a netted terminal. Add an edging, if desired.

2 Work a connection weave with one end, working the warp only, to create a "T" intersection a few inches (cm) up from the end.

TERMINAL

3 Work a tombstone terminal on the second end. Cut pieces of the leather larger than the width of the strap and the netted terminal. Cover the surface of the leather with glue. Lay the second piece of leather on top of the first. Weight down and allow the glue to dry.

4 Cut the leather to the width of the strap and then use a circle template to trace the rounded shape onto the leather.

5 Following the manufacturer's instructions, set a grommet into the center of the tombstone terminal.

6 Use split ring pliers to open the key ring and slide it onto the terminal, gently pushing the ring around until the key ring is completely through the grommet.

7 Slide the catch on the large end of the lanyard onto the ring.

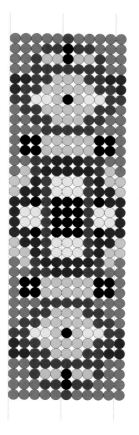

See additional bead graphs on page 136.

Lolita

When you need to make a quick lipstick check, pull this beaded mirror out of your purse.

beading materials

- ½ tube of each color 11/0 seed beads
- ½ tube 14/0 seed beads (optional)
- Needle
- Thread

other materials

- Leather
- Heavy-duty interfacing
- 1- to 2-inch (2.5 to 5 cm) mirror
- Piece of paper
- Alcohol
- Glue (flexible/stretchable)
- Needle
- Thread

tools

- Loom
- Craft knife
- Pencil
- Ruler

techniques

- Taped or woven terminal (page 28)
- Connect the dots (page 37)
- Rolled edging (page 36)
- Whipstitch beaded corner (page 41)

instructions

1 Weave the mirror backing following the graph. Work a taped or woven terminal at each end. Work the connect-the-dot surface embellishment.

2 Use the beadwork as a template to cut two squares of the leather or ultra suede and one of the interfacing. Trim the interfacing ¼ inch (6 mm) on two sides to make it ⅛ inch (3 mm) smaller than the backing material.

3 Glue the mirror to the interfacing following the manufacturer's instructions.

4 Choose a design and cut out the window opening.

SNOWFLAKE OPENING

Cut a square of paper smaller than the mirror backing. Fold it in half two times. Beginning on the fold, cut out an odd-shaped opening. Unfold the paper, and tape it to the square of backing material. Use a craft knife to cut out the pattern. Clean the mirror surface with alcohol. Brush a small amount of glue onto the back side of the square of backing material around the edges of the material. Carefully center the square on the mirror, and glue. Cover with a piece of paper to protect the surface, weight with a beanbag, and allow to dry.

FLIP TOP OPENING (Shown)

On the back side of the square backing material, use the ruler to draw lines around the square, ½ inch (1.3 cm) in from each edge. Use the craft knife and ruler to cut an "X" through the center of the square. Work a picot edging along the lines of the "X." Once the mirror is edged, fold the flaps back and sew in place using beads to decorate the surface.

5 Sandwich the layers of the mirror together, and then baste the edges of the material in place, forming an envelope around the backed mirror. Work a rolled edging around all four sides.

Latitudes Belt

Accent your hourglass figure
with this slim beaded belt.

beading materials

- Tube or hank of 11/0 beads for each color in the graph
- Beading needle
- Beading thread

other materials

- Cotton webbing, 1 inch (2.5 cm) wide and at least 5 inches (12.7 cm) longer than the desired belt length
- Thread to match webbing color
- Belt buckle

tools

- Tape measure
- Loom longer than the length of your belt (42-inch [106.7 cm] loom)
- Sewing needle
- Scissors

techniques

- Taped or woven terminal (page 28)
- Whipstitch (page 41)

photo 1

photo 2

instructions

1 Measure the recipient's waist. Weave the beads according to your chosen pattern until you reach the measurement. The buckle will add enough length for the belt to fit comfortably. Make a taped or woven terminal.

2 Sew the beadwork to the webbing using a whipstitch and folding the terminals under.

3 Trim each end of the webbing 1 1/2 inches (3.8 cm) longer than the beaded strap.

4 Fold each end of the webbing under so the raw edges are tucked inside, and then stitch in place. Push a sewn end through the clasp of the buckle, and fold it over the bail. After making sure the sides are neat and even, sew to secure (see photos 1 and 2).

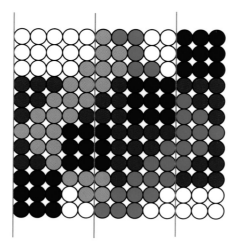

See additional bead graphs on page 137.

Kachina Zipper Pull

Snap this colorful pull onto a
backpack zipper for quick access
or to dress up your winter parka.

beading materials

- Small amounts of 11/0 seed bead
- Beading needle
- Beading thread

other materials

- Painter's tape
- Small scraps of leather
- Glue or contact cement
- Grommet
- Lanyard finding

tools

- Loom
- Scissors
- Circle template
- Grommet setter
- Hole punch

techniques

- Netted or woven terminal (page 29)
- Warp weave (page 28)
- Picot edging (page 34)
- Short strand fringe (page 38)

instructions

1 Work a strip of beadwork five, seven, or nine beads wide by 2 to 8 inches (5 to 20.3 cm) long. Work a netted or woven terminal on one end and woven warps on the other.

2 Place a strip of blue painter's tape over two pieces of scrap leather. Use a template to draw ½-inch (1.3 cm) circles onto the tape. Cut out the circles.

3 Place a drop of glue or cement onto the circles. Rub the circles together to distribute the glue evenly, and pull them apart. Sandwich the netted terminal between the two circles. Weight with sandbag, and allow the glue to set.

figure 1

4 Once the glue is dry, trim the threads and add a grommet.

5 With a new thread, work a picot edging around the leather circle, beginning next to the edge of the beaded strip and ending on the opposite side. Refer to the strings that are blue in figure 1.

6 Using the same thread, string a short fringe on the last two beads you added in the picot edging. String a bead between each of the picot points.

7 Work a second fringe on the last two beads of the picot edging on this side (shown in red in figure 1). Tie off and trim the thread.

8 Attach a lanyard clasp through the grommet. If you use a small clasp, you can bend the end of the clasp outward to widen it and then bend it back in place with pliers.

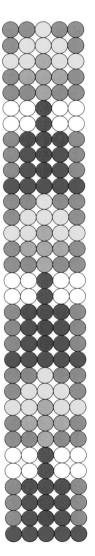

See additional bead graphs on page 138.

Open Sesame Keychains

Start with a simple beaded strap, and then add fringe and embellishments to make a modish keychain.

beading materials

- Hank or tube of 11/0 beads for each color in the graph
- Needle
- Thread

other materials

- Key ring
- Small strip of leather
- Glue or contact cement

tools

- Short loom
- Scissors
- Beanbags

techniques

- Warp weave (page 28)
- Pointed terminal (page 30)
- Bail terminal (page 27)

instructions

WEAVING

1 Weave a strap of beadwork following the graph. Work a blunt terminal at the top and a pointed or blunt one on the bottom end.

TERMINALS

2 Warp-weave the bottom terminal. For the top, work a netted terminal on the innermost 10 warps, and warp-weave the four warps on either side. Trim the netted terminal to about ¾ inch (1.9 cm).

LEATHER BAIL

3 Trim the leather so it is slightly wider than the netted terminal at the top of the beaded strap. Fold the leather in half, and taper the sides slightly so the top of the folded strip is narrower than the bottom ends. Pass one end of the leather piece through a key ring. Place contact cement

or glue on the ends and glue them over the netted terminal, leaving the middle of the strip unglued. Use beanbags to weight it down and allow for the glue to set up, following the manufacturer's instructions.

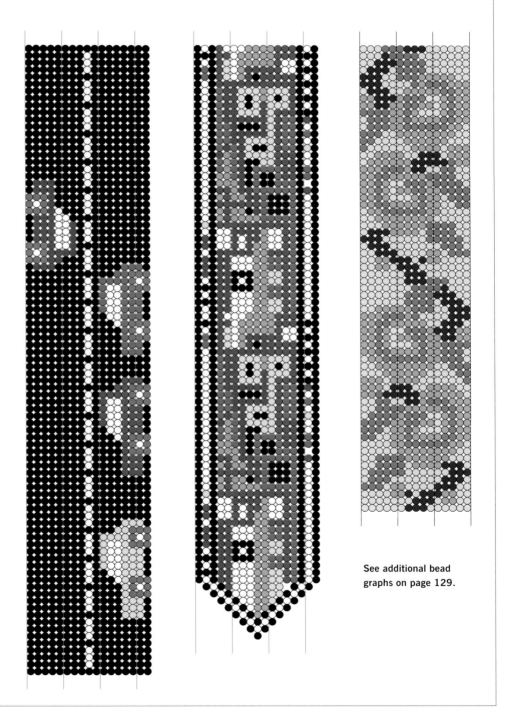

See additional bead graphs on page 129.

MP3 Pouch

Free up valuable purse and pocket
space with a beaded leather
pouch for your MP3 player.

beading materials

- Hank or tube of 11/0 beads in each color on the graph
- Needle
- Beading thread
- Sturdy lobster claw clasp
- 3 split rings

other materials

- Leather scraps
- Sewing needle
- Sewing thread
- 1/2-inch (1.3 cm) length of hook-and-loop fastener or a hook-and-loop circle

techniques

- Pointed terminal (page 30)
- Whipstitch (page 41)
- Attaching metal findings (page 32)

photo 2

instructions

THE POUCH

1 Measure the width, height, and depth of your MP3 player. Cut a strip of leather 2¹/₂ times as long as the height and the depth, and 1 inch (2.5 cm) wider. Fold in half, right sides together, so the fold is at the bottom. Sew along the long sides using a ¹/₄-inch (6 mm) seam allowance. Sew a perpendicular seam at each corner to make the depth for the bottom of the pouch (photo 1).

BEADWORK AND ARMATURE

2 Bead a strap 1 inch (2.5 cm) shorter than the leather cut in step 1. Work a pointed terminal, leaving the two center warp threads for a clasp.

3 Cut a strip of leather the width of the beadwork and about 1 inch (2.5 cm) longer. Center the beadwork on the strip, and sew it down using the whipstitch. Trim the extra leather at each end to match the pointed terminal of the beadwork.

CLASP

4 Add a split ring to a lobster claw clasp. Work the loop with the two center warp threads, adding the split ring on with the beads. Do the same to make the catch, except add a split ring to a second split ring.

5 Using a spider wire or other strong thread, reinforce the loop by passing the thread through the beads of the loop and tying it off in a discreet way in the leather (photo 2).

photo 1

MP3 Pouch

ATTACHING THE BEADWORK

6 Leaving ¼ unglued, add glue along the remaining ¾ of the beaded armature, and position it carefully on the pouch. Let dry according to the manufacturer's instructions. The unglued section will be a "holster strap" for the headset.

7 Once it's dry, secure the armature by stitching along the sides at each end where it's glued. Trim the pouch to match the angled shape of the pointed terminal.

HEADSET HOLSTER

8 Add a piece of hook-and-loop fastener at the terminal of the armature and in the corresponding spot on the pouch.

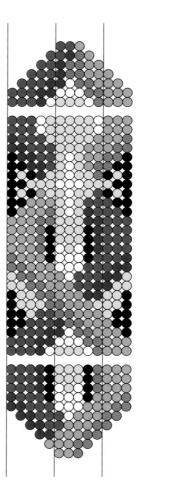

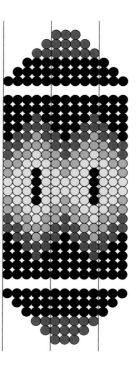

See additional bead graphs on page 139.

appendix

READING GRAPHS

Following are some tips for reading and using the graphs and legends that come with the projects in this book.

Legends, Guide Lines, and Spaces

Pattern colors are indicated in the legend that accompanies each graph. To help you keep track of any color changes you decide to make, and to ease color transitions, mark the new colors on a copy of the legend. Graphs are worked in sections to create different parts of the beadwork—specifically, repetitive motifs with terminals that end the work in a special way. Some graphs include vertical guidelines to make counting the beads easier as you work. These divide the graphs into five-bead sections. (Depending on the width of the project, a section along the edge may include fewer than five beads.)

Other guidelines indicate special instructions in a pattern; for example, thread paths for edgings, as in the Aztec Sky light-switch cover on page 90, or the weft edging on the Endless Straps on page 60.

Spaces between sections of a graph indicate special-effect changes in the weaving pattern.

Mixing and Matching Patterns

Many of the projects in this book are designed for mix-and-match selections from their graphs. For example, if you'd like to weave a bracelet or cuff with the pattern provided for a napkin ring or even a guitar strap, simply use the graph you like, adapting the terminals to your size and adding a clasp; or, if you really like a bracelet pattern and want to add it to a wider project, follow the bracelet color pattern, adding enough beads on either side as you work to make it fit the width of your project.

Manipulating and Printing Graphs

Sometimes graphs in books are awkward to follow: you have to struggle to keep the book open at the right page, or the graph is so small it can't be read (by those of us over 40, anyway) without poking your nose right up to the page. To solve these problems, just photocopy the pattern—or scan and print it at normal or high quality—enlarging it as desired.

To change the color scheme of a pattern, print the graph at draft quality or lighten it even more with your computer's software to give the printed pattern a faded look. Then use colored pencils or markers to fill in the "beads" with the colors you'd rather use.

Orienting Patterns

Each graph is presented top to bottom on the printed page, but how you read your graph will depend on whether you work your beads on a horizontal or vertical loom. Since I prefer horizontal looms, I position my graphs with their tops turned to the left, and I read the rows, which now run vertically, from left to right. When I work on a vertical loom, I position the graph top up, and read the rows from top to bottom. If you work your rows from the bottom upward, you'll read your graphs from the bottom to the top.

twisted warp bracelet

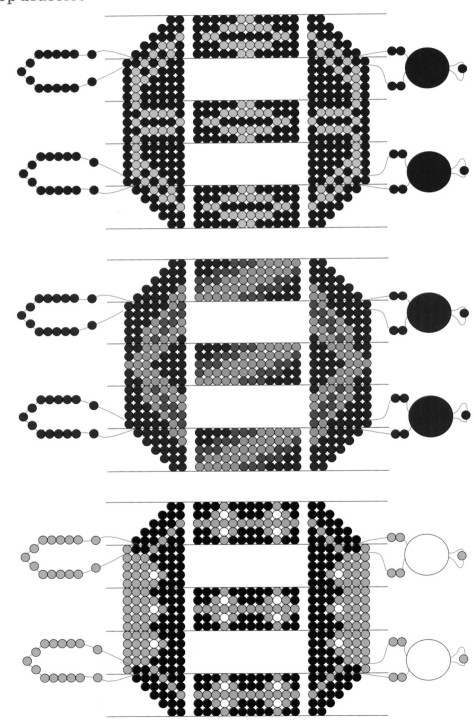

tag bracelet

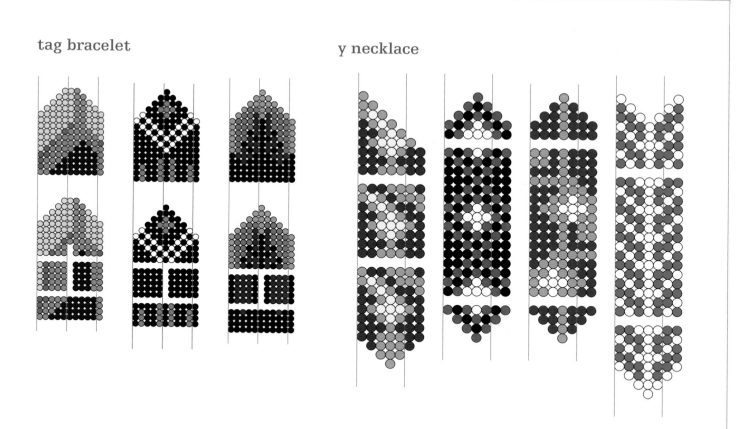

y necklace

cantina set

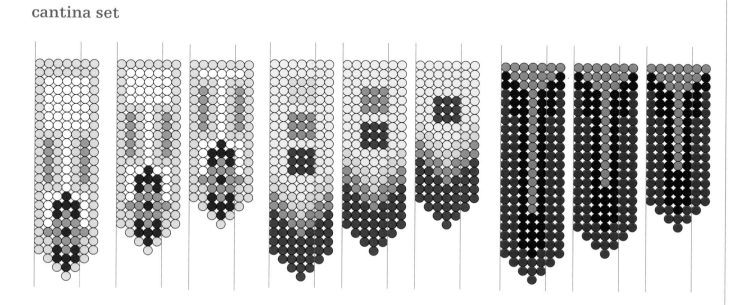

windowpane bracelet

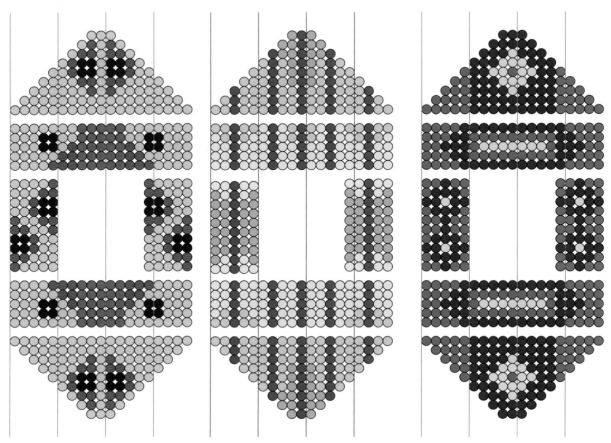

free spirit pin

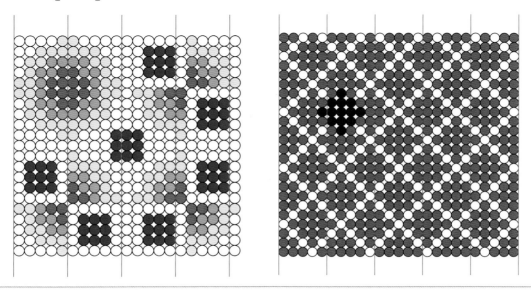

bestseller

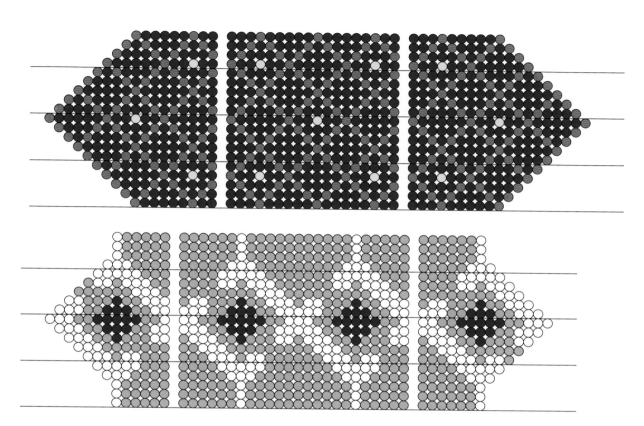

free spirit pin

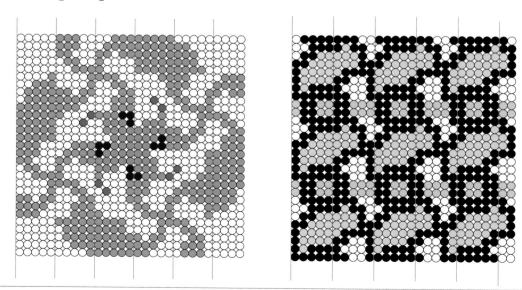

bestseller, light pull, and key chains

aztec sky

stellular

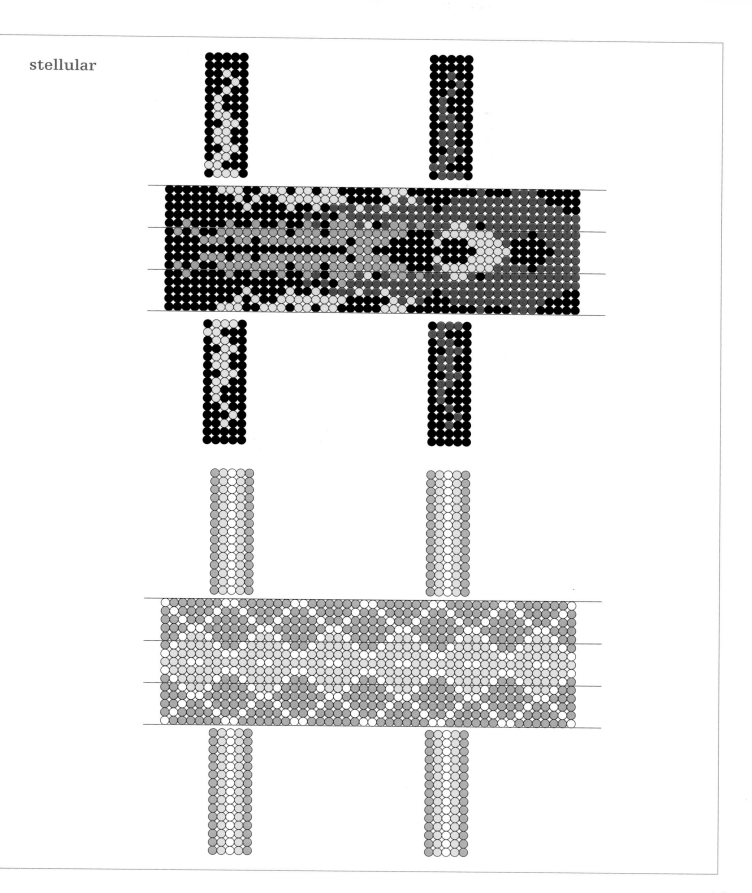

trailblazer

guitar strap

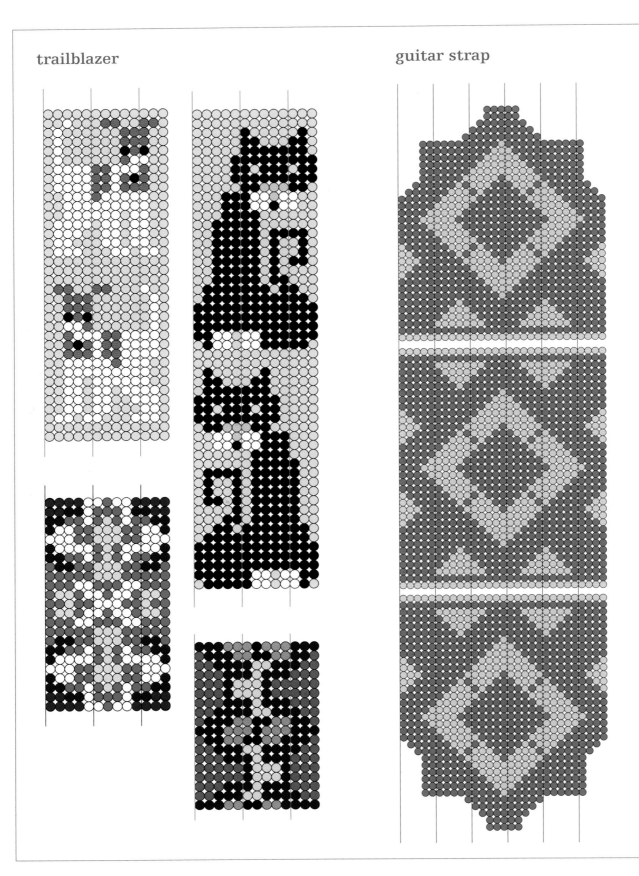

guitar strap

rio card holder

amulet bag

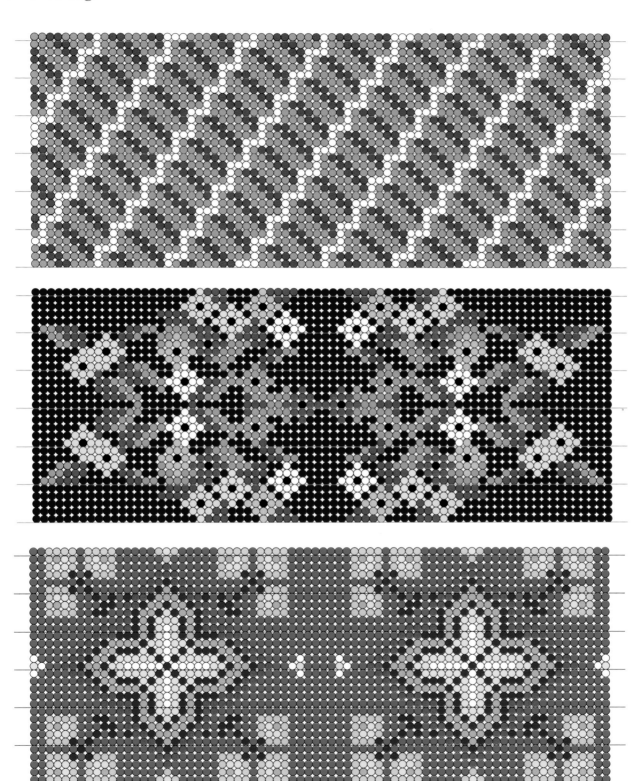

canyon lands

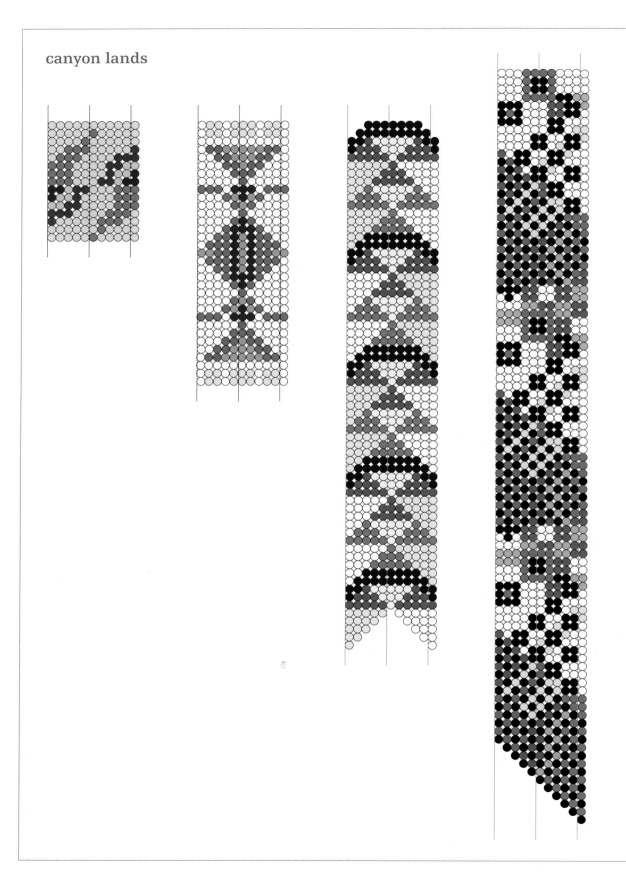

durango and latitudes belts

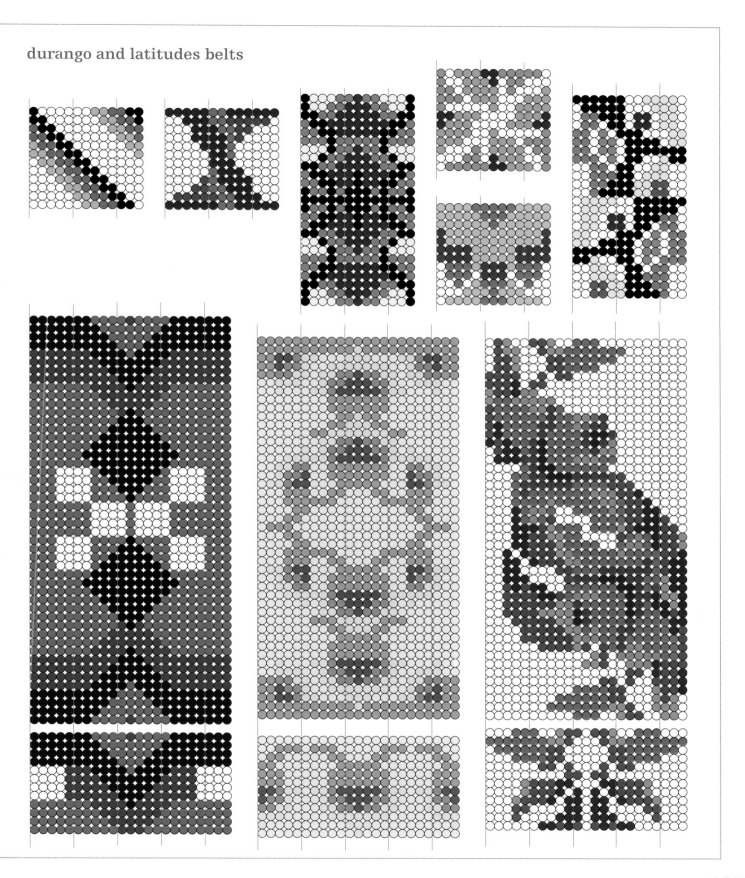

endless strap, light shade skirt, and kachina zipper pull

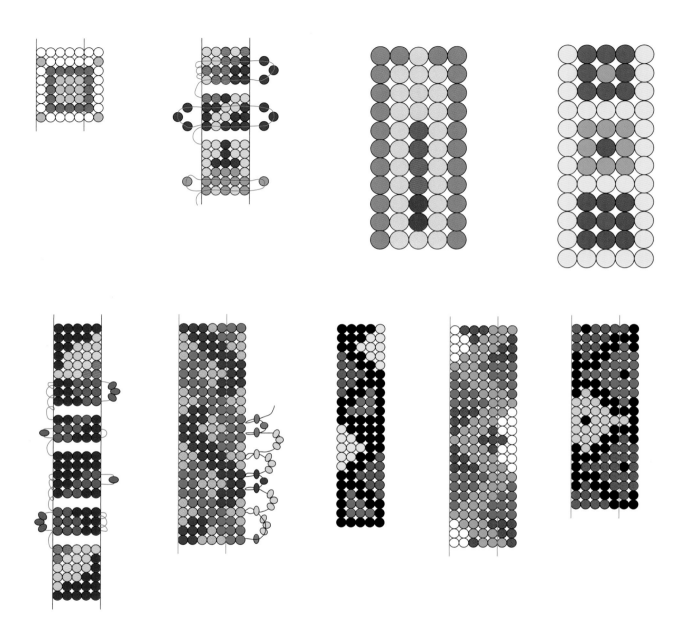

MP3 pouch

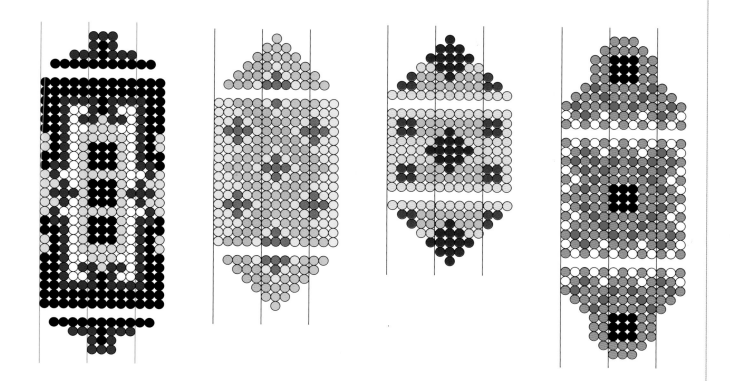

MAKE YOUR OWN LOOMS

Making a Pin Loom

The pin loom described here is designed for the patterns in this book. To alter its size for your own designs, just cut the foam board to the desired dimensions and use more pins, as needed. Add enough pins to hold the required number of warp threads, plus two extra threads for anchoring the thread at the end. For example, a project that is 11 beads wide will require 12 warps and 14 pins.

TOOLS
- Craft knife
- Straight edge
- Materials
- Foam board
- Two-sided tape
- Corsage pins

1. Cut a strip of foam board 3 inches (7.6 cm) wide, and 18 to 24 inches (45.7 to 61 cm) long.

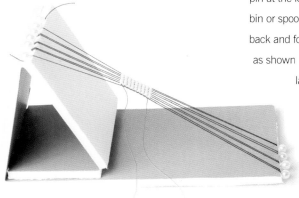

2. In order to fold the strip into the pin-loom shape shown in the photo, you'll need to score it in three places. Start by measuring and marking three lines across the strip, 2 inches (5 cm), 7 inches (17.8 cm), and 15 inches (38.1 cm) from one end. Then, at these marked lines, score only through the top layer of the foam board.

3. Fold the foam board at the scored lines, and use two-sided tape to secure the triangular shape to the base.

4. Push corsage pins into the top edge of the foam and into the edge of the base, using as many as required for the desired number of warp threads. (The pins will serve as both anchors and spacers.) To make it easier to remove the work from the loom, place two more pins in the top bridge than in the bottom bridge so that you can secure the tail without knotting the thread.

5. To warp the loom, you'll start with the top pin at the left. Tie an end of thread from a bobbin or spool onto that first pin. Warp the thread back and forth, catching the thread on the pins as shown in the photo. When you reach the last two pins, wrap the thread three times around the first pin and push the pin firmly down into the foam. Wrap three times in the opposite direction around the last pin, and push it down into the foam, too. This should secure the thread in place.

6. To work the weft on a pin loom, start by threading a stop bead. Use a blunt needle; it's very important not to pierce any of the warp threads as you work. You'll also want to avoid knots, so use ample thread.

7. Work the first row, leaving the spacing of the warps as they are for now. You'll tighten them up after weaving the third row.

8. Work two more rows with the wide, unevenly spaced warp threads.

9. Pull the weft threads tight by tugging on the tail at the left of the warp.

10. Work the length of woven weft required for your project.

11. Pull the bottom left-hand pin out to free the first two warp threads.

12. Pull the second warp thread up to reduce the size of the loop until it rests next to the first bead; this will free the second loop (the second and third threads) from its pin (see figure 1).

figure 1

13. Continue pulling the loops of warp up to the beads, working loop by loop as they are loosened from their pins. Because most threads are twisted, the last warp thread may try to twist up on itself. Placing your finger inside the loop as you pull will keep the tension on it and keep the strands separated until the loop is in place. Loosen the tail and untwist the last warp thread.

14. Weave the tails at the beginning and end of the weft into the work (see page 23).

Making Wood Looms

Making a wood loom is fairly easy, but you'll either need to have the pieces cut at your local hardware store, or cut the pieces yourself with hand or power tools. Larger stores will do the cutting for you at a minimal charge. You can even piece a loom together using scrap lumber.

SLEIGH LOOM

Like commercial sleigh looms, this simple loom consists of a body and two bridges with spacers.

TOOLS

- Saw
- Drill with $1/8$-inch (3 mm) bit
- Screwdriver

MATERIALS

- Pine, hemlock, or maple board, the width desired for your loom
- Four 2-inch (5 cm) wood screws
- A few $1/2$-inch (1.3 cm) screws for extra anchors, if desired
- 2 springs, slightly shorter than the width of the board
- 4 screws, each $1/2$ inch (1.3 cm) long or a fine-toothed comb, some masking tape, and a craft knife
- Sandpaper
- Wood glue
- Gloves

1. Cut two 4-inch-long (10.2 cm) end pieces from the lumber. If you want your loom to sit horizontally, cut off one corner of each piece at an angle.

2. Cut the body of the loom at least 8 inches (20.3 cm) longer than the beadwork to be woven.

3. Sand all the pieces smooth.

4. Each end piece will be fastened to an end of the body with two screws. To keep the wood from cracking when you tighten down these screws, first predrill two holes through each end piece and into the ends of the body.

5. Apply a small amount of wood glue to the areas of the end and body that will be joined. Attach the three pieces with the screws, leaving the screw heads raised slightly to serve as anchors. Let the glue dry.

6. To attach spring spacers, start by pre-drilling a hole at each end of one bridge. Bend the loop at each end of the spring downward so that it's perpendicular to the rest of the spring. Secure one end of the spring to the bridge with a $1/2$-inch (1.3 cm) screw. While wearing gloves to prevent the spring from pinching your fingers, stretch the spring until the other end loop is even with the second hole, and attach that loop with the other $1/2$-inch (1.3 cm) screw. Repeat to attach the other spring to the other bridge.

To create notched spacers, use masking tape to attach a fine-toothed comb along the top edge of one bridge. Then place the blade of a craft knife between the teeth, and push down firmly to form a notch. Work notches along the entire length of the bridge. Remove the comb, and repeat along the top edge of the other bridge.

OJIBWA-STYLE LOOM

This is a quick and easy loom to make. It's named after a similar loom that the Ojibwa tribe invented and used.

TOOLS

- Saw
- Drill with a $3/8$-inch (9.5 mm) drill bit
- Fine-toothed comb

MATERIALS

- 2 lengths of 1 x 4 lumber, in the desired widths of the bridges. (If you want the loom to sit horizontally, cut off one corner of each piece at an angle.)
- 2 lengths of $3/8$-inch (9.5 mm) wooden dowel, cut 8 inches (20.3 cm) longer than the desired length of the loom
- Piece of scrap wood
- Sandpaper
- Wood glue
- Rag
- Masking tape
- Craft knife

1. Cut each of the dowels to 10 inches (25.4 cm) longer than the length of the beadwork to be made.

2. Tape the two 1 x 4 pieces together, aligning their edges, and place them on top of a piece of scrap wood. Drill two $3/8$-inch-diameter (9.5 mm) holes all the way through them. (The scrap wood will support the two pieces and will minimize splintering as the drill bit bores through the wood.)

3. Sand all the pieces smooth. Check the fit of the wooden dowels in the drilled holes; they should slide in smoothly but snugly. If necessary, sand the dowels until they fit. If they're too loose, you can use wooden toothpicks as wedges in the next step.

4. Apply a small amount of wood glue to the inner surfaces of the holes and slide the dowels into them, leaving their ends poking out about 2 inches (5 cm). These extended ends will serve as anchors. Use a damp rag to wipe away excess glue.

5. Use the comb to make notched spacers along the top edge of each bridge. (See step 6 on page 141.)

acknowledgments

It is a great pleasure to acknowledge the following people:

The staff of Lark Books who have been an absolute joy to work with. My friend and husband, Robert Bateman, who was very patient and kind through this whole process (even when my beads migrated onto his toast) and who was a great help making the many looms I experimented with.

My niece, Kelly Hames, who helped test the patterns. Thanks, sweetie! You are a peach!

My friend, Lucy Elle, who helped by reviewing the patterns and making a few of the loom pieces to help me when I was particularly busy.

My friend, Jan Wasser, for testing looms and being patient with this horrible hermit.

And last but not least my grandchildren: Alexander, Angela, and Gabriel. You are all really short and you smell funny, but you're all so darn cute that I think, perhaps, we can put up with you.

about the author

Sharon Bateman is a mixed-media artist best known for her many magazine articles, appearances on DIY's *Jewelry Making* show, and beading books that include *Findings and Finishings* (Interweave Press, 2003) as well as her self-published titles *Morning Rose Rosette* (2001), *Peepers and Creepers* (2000), and *Over the Edge* (2005). Sharon invented and manufactures Sharondipity Tube Looms—clear plastic looms designed for specific projects. She is available for questions or comments at www.sharonbateman.com.

index